C.A. BUSBY

The Regency Architect of Brighton & Hove

Neil Bingham

This book is published to coincide with the exhibition of the same name held at the RIBA Heinz Gallery, 13 March to 27 April 1991, and at the Royal Brighton Pavilion, Art Gallery and Museum, Brighton, 9 August to 6 October 1991.

RIBA Heinz Gallery 1991

ISBN: 1 872911 10 2

Affectionately dedicated to my mother, Brighton-born

EX LIBRIS POOLE

ACKNOWLEDGMENTS FOR ILLUSTRATIONS

All illustrations, with the exception of the following, are reproduced by permission of the RIBA Drawings Collection. In addition I would like to thank: Colour plate I & Fig.15 The Board of Trustees of the Victoria and Albert Museum; Figs.13 & 14 City of Bristol Record Office; Colour plate V The Earl of Normanton; Colour plate VI The National Library of Wales; Fig.20 The Historical Society of Pennsylvania; Fig.21 Sotheby's; Fig.30 The Library of Congress; Fig.31 The Trustees of Sir John Soane's Museum; Fig.35 The Royal Society of Arts; Figs.40 & 59 Private collection; Figs.41 & 47 Royal Commission on the Historical Monuments of England; Fig.44 Brighton Central Reference Library; Figs.36, 45 & 48 The Royal Pavilion, Art Gallery and Museum, Brighton; Fig.53(right half) James Griffith. The following photographs are by the author: Colour plates III, IX & XI and Figs.2, 6, 8, 9, 10, 37, 38, 42, 50, 51, 58, 60, 66, 69, 72 & 73.

Front cover: Unexecuted design for houses on the "West Cliff", Brighton, c1825 (detail).
Back cover: Balcony design from C.A. Busby's *A Collection of Designs for Modern Embellishments*, c1810.

CONTENTS

FOREWORD BY SIR JOHN SUMMERSON

Up to now, the work of C.A. Busby has been known in the world of architectural scholarship by only two examples: the Commercial Rooms in Corn Street, Bristol and some sets of houses in Brighton. The first, a refined and subtle piece of Neo-classicism, was illustrated (and, alas, misattributed) by Professor Richardson in his seminal Monumental Classic Architecture in Great Britain and Ireland during the 18th and 19th Centuries of 1914; the second, more robust and adventurous, were brought to notice by Antony Dale in his Fashionable Brighton of 1947. These buildings show an interesting and original mind at work and it was with pleasurable anticipation that one learned of the acquisition by the Royal Institute of British Architects in 1986 of close to two hundred drawings by this almost forgotten architect of the Regency decade and its afterglow.

These drawings form the core of the present exhibition and, with additions from other sources and a great deal of original research by Neil Bingham, give a very adequate picture of Busby's professional achievements. Nobody is going to claim that he was the greatest architect of his age, but he had talent and a strong wish to do new things, technological as well as stylistic. Dr Bingham has followed him to America where Busby seems to have cut a figure of some interest. His English works, including the two pattern-books, contain some surprising novelties. Busby is a Regency personality worth meeting and Neil Bingham affords us a ready opportunity of doing so.

ACKNOWLEDGEMENTS

When I first arrived to work at the Drawings Collection of the Royal Institute of British Architects in 1986, Jill Lever, then Deputy Curator, asked if I would like to catalogue the recently acquired collection of drawings by C.A. Busby (1786-1834). It must have been fate. Having just returned to England after a year in my native Canada, I had moved to Brighton. It was a town I knew in a paradoxical manner, only vaguely from my few visits to my great-aunt Vi in the previous several years, but intimately from the stories of my mother who had been born in Brighton and raised there as a child before being taken to live on the Canadian prairies. My mother brought me up to believe that Brighton was the most beautiful place in the world. She was, of course, right. And now I had been given the opportunity of researching one of the principal reasons that Brighton is so beautiful - Busby's architecture.

Before the RIBA purchased the Busby drawings - with a generous grant from the National Art Collections Fund - the 200 or so sheets had been in the family possession of a descendant of Francis Wells, who by tradition is believed to have been a pupil of Busby's. Considered of little importance, the drawings had remained undisturbed until an architect had alerted the RIBA to their existence.

Many of the drawings are an odd shape; Busby had taken a pair of scissors to them and cut away stained areas following their being damaged by water, probably due to a house flood. On some of the drawings he made pencilled notes of the subjects; fortunately for me or I might never have traced them.

The newly discovered drawings acted as catalysts to my research. With a research grant from the British Academy - whom I would like to thank - I was able to follow in Busby's footsteps through Britain and America.

Antony Dale's work Fashionable Brighton, first published in 1947, contained a wealth of new material on Busby's Brighton buildings. I am pleased to have had the opportunity to supplement this pioneering study and to clarify such facts as that Busby's partner was Amon Henry Wilds, not his father Amon Wilds, and that Busby's middle name was

Augustin, not Augustus. I would like to thank Mr Dale for generously giving me his time to discuss Busby.

In Brighton I happened upon Nick Tyson and Margaret Bass, both of whom I can only describe as "Busby-mad". For the last several years they have devoted their lives to making a painstakingly accurate restoration of their Busby house in Brunswick Square. Nick kindly acted as my local researcher, helping me sift through and identify drawings of buildings in Brunswick Town.

The staff of the Royal Pavilion, Art Gallery and Museum of Brighton have also been invaluably helpful, and I owe a particular obligation to John Roles and Philip Vainker.

Michael Ray, Chief Planner for Hove, pointed out several helpful sources for information on Brunswick Town, which lies under his sympathetic jurisdiction. And for their knowledgable assistance I would like to thank Robert Gregory; Christoper Whittock, County Archivist for East Sussex; and Nick Savage, Assistant Librarian of the Royal Academy of Arts.

I am happy to acknowledge the willing and courteous help I have received from the staffs of many libraries and other institutions where I have researched, particularly the Brighton Reference Library and the New-York Historical Society.

My colleagues at the Drawings Collection have been extremely understanding. It is always a pleasure working with them. My biggest thanks goes to our Curator Jill Lever (herself raised in Busby's Kemp Town, no less) for introducing me to the Busby drawings and for her constant encouragement and helpful advice. Jane Preger, Exhibitions Officer, not only put this small book together, but helped me organise the Busby exhibition. Charlotte Podro, our Conservator, mended the damaged drawings in her usual highly skilled manner. Andy Norris, Tim Knox and Sian Williams having always been there to help.

This publication and the accompanying exhibition have been generously funded by a grant made by American Express. Their support seems particularly apt because Busby lived on Wall Street in New York (well before it had any connection with the financial world), and Brighton is the home of the European operating centre for American Express.

Finally, my thanks to Dr Lynne Walker, Dr Giles Worsley and Lady Wedgwood for their helpful suggestions and to my friend Jonathan Hoyle for his emotional support.

I
Charles Augustin Busby, aged 21, painted by the portrait miniaturist J. Fruman, July 1807.

II
Section of the unexecuted design for the Court House and Butter Market, Croydon, Surrey, 1806. An early example of Busby's fine draughtsmanship.

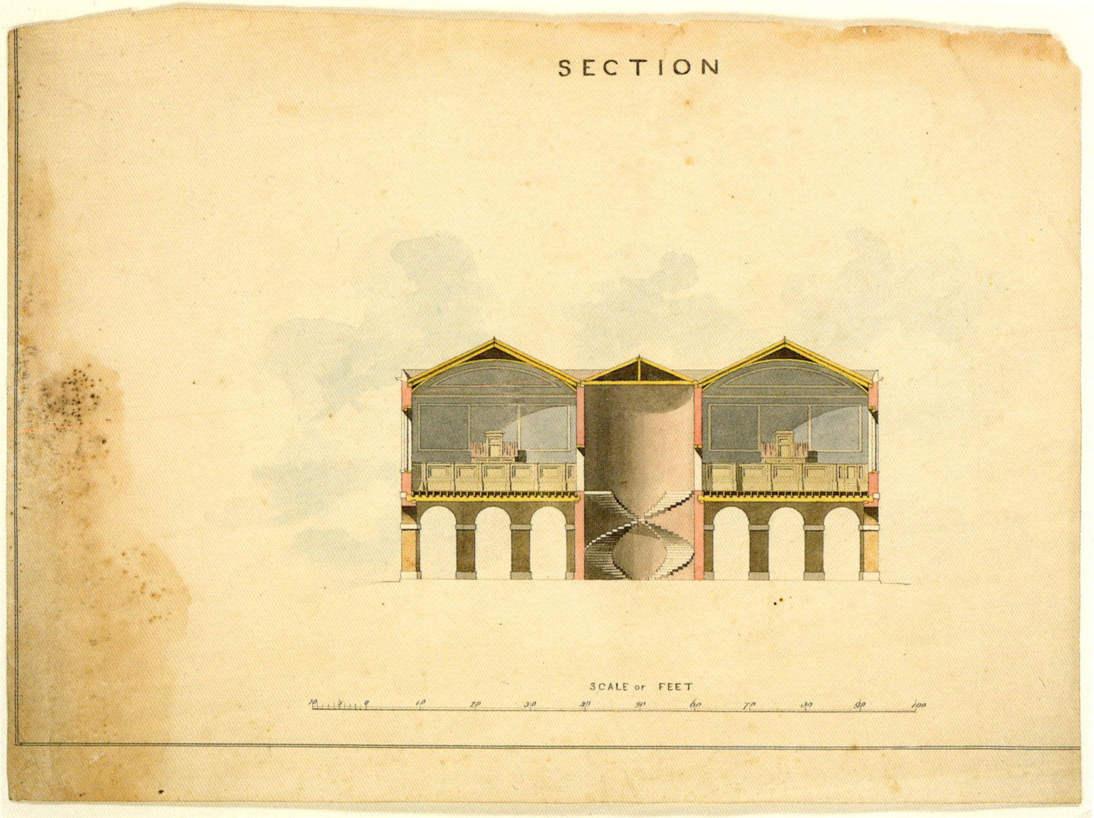

III
The lantern with caryatids over the principal room of the Commercial Coffee Rooms, Bristol.

IV
Patent design for a lock system for the Regent's Canal, 1813. Busby claimed that his design solved the problem of the great volume of water lost by conventional lock methods.

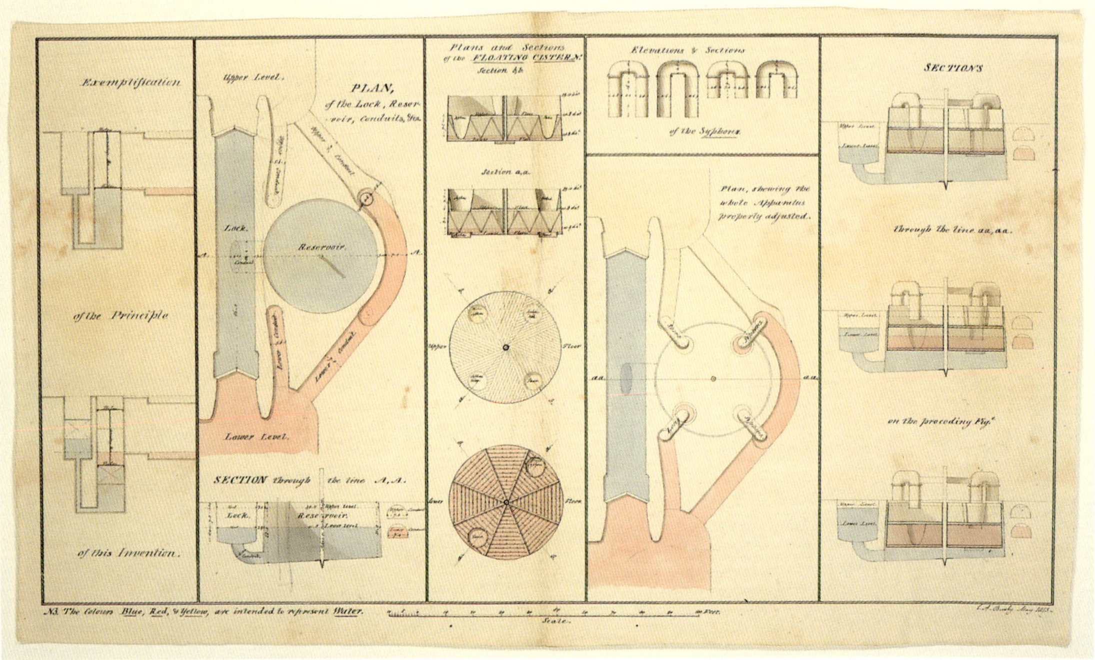

V
The pheasantry and keeper's cottage at Somerley, Hampshire, 1814. A picturesque garden building with a central cottage, cages on either side, and shaded seats at each end.

For Henry Baring Esq. M.P.   C. A. Busby Archt. Mar 1814

Lloyd Bamford Hesketh Esqr.

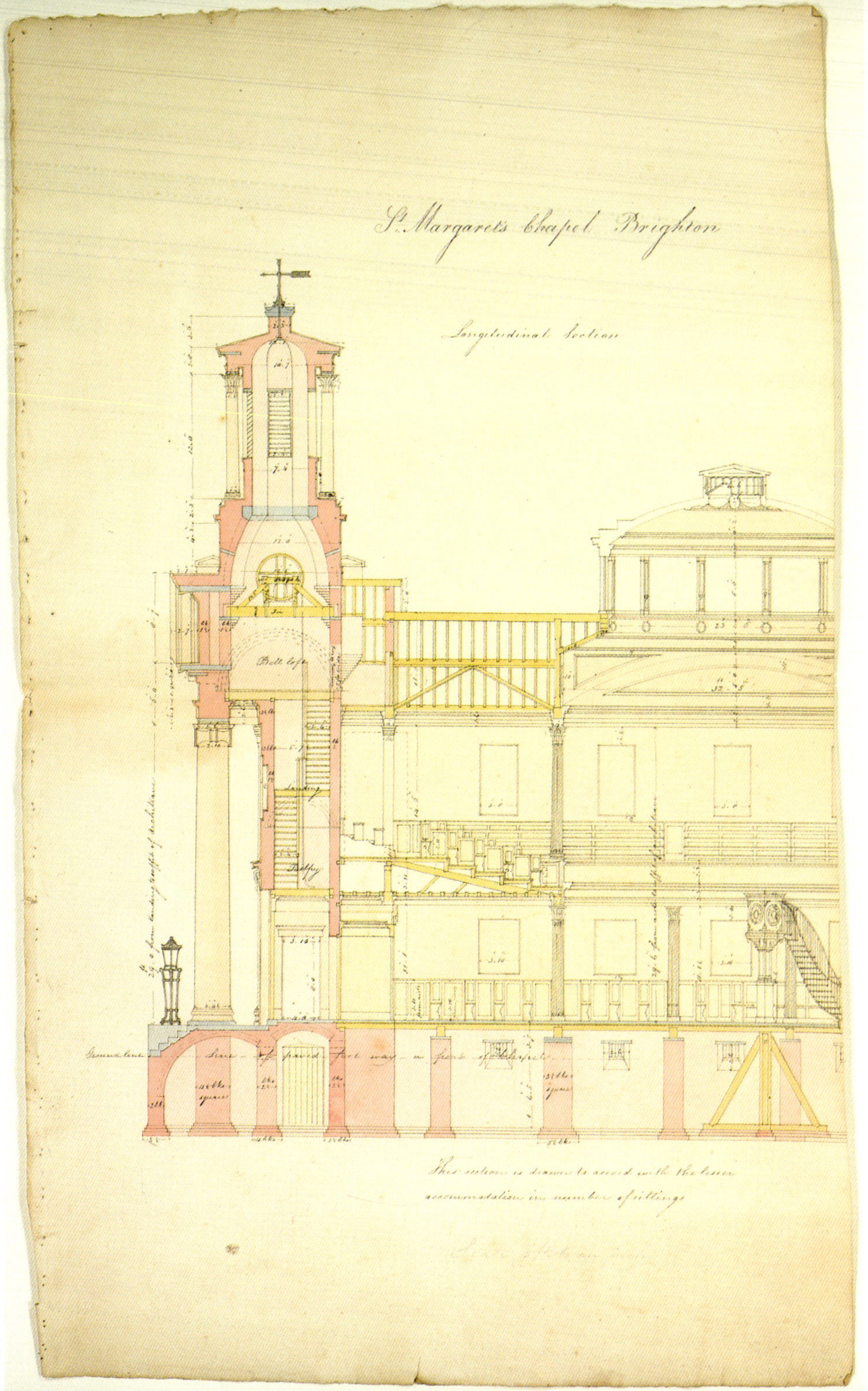

VI
Perspective of Gwrych Castle, near Abergele, Wales, 1814. Busby's "sublime" design was subsequently reworked by the architect Thomas Rickman and the owner L.B. Hesketh.

VII
Longitudinal section of a working drawing for the Church of St Margaret, Brighton, *c*1824.

VIII
A large oak bookcase in the gothic style for the Rev Dr Holland, 1823.

IX
The west side of Brunswick Square.

X
Elevation, almost as executed, for one of the houses at Nos.26 to 33 Brunswick Square, almost as built, *c*1825.

XI
Nos.30 to 33 Brunswick Square.

XII
Design for a shop front. An experiment by Busby in design and construction.

INTRODUCTION

Busby's finest creations are the handsome seaside crescents and terraces of Kemp Town in Brighton - which he designed with his short-term partner, A.H. Wilds - and Brunswick Town in neighbouring Hove. Mainly built during the 1820s, these works are therefore not strictly 'Regency' in period, which by definition is confined to the years between 1811 and 1820; but as the term is generally applied to the span approximately between 1790 and 1840, it seems pedantic not to consider Busby's Brighton and Hove architecture as Regency, although in his late designs the heavier elements of the William IV style are in evidence.

And anyway, it would be difficult to find another architect who asserted such strong interests in so many characteristic aspects of the Regency period: in the new materials and mechanical devices born of the Industrial Revolution; in the aesthetic tug-of-war between the picturesque and the sublime; in the emergence of the latest architectural styles, especially the Greek Revival; in interior decoration; and in the opportunities in town planning. During his career Busby designed buildings of almost every major type: small country houses, villas and town houses; churches and chapels; shops; coffee houses, theatres, assembly and ballrooms; prisons and courthouses. So strong were Busby's associations with what he referred to as "the science of architecture", which in his own work ranged from locks, canals, and bridge construction to the creation of such marvellous inventions as steam-powered paddleboats and hydraulic orreries, that Busby called himself an architect-engineer. His was the last generation to be able to do so, before the polarisation of the professions set in; the year Busby died, for example, also saw the founding of the Institute of British Architects.

Characteristic for the period dominated by the aftermath of the North American and European revolutions, C.A. Busby was a political activist, a strong proponent of liberal reform. He had a fighting spirit, and his outspokeness on matters of equity and justice, which often involved him personally, plunged him into controversy on several occasions. His political views quite naturally coloured his view of architecture and its social rôle; he considered his experiments in prison design as serving as instruments to change and reform. And although Busby is chiefly remembered as the architect of upper-class housing in Brighton, he himself shunned the Whig inhabitants who danced at the Court of the Prince of Wales. Busby's name never appeared on the guest-list of the Royal Pavilion.

Busby's career experienced the highs and lows of the Regency age. As a young architect and engineer studying and practising during the first decade and a half of the 19th century,

Busby was barred by the Continental wars from studying French and Italian architecture which were important in many an architect's development. When the conflicts were finally resolved around 1815, he chose not to travel to Europe, like most of his contemporaries, but to go to the United States, a tell-tale sign of his quest for the new and experimental. And it had been the experimental that had driven him there, his career having taken a turn for the worse when one of his innovative roof designs led to a structural collapse. This penchant for scientific enquiry helped but more often hindered his fortunes, and in conjunction with the swings in the building and property markets, Busby's finances were often in a dire state. Only during the height of Brighton's property speculation in the mid-1820s, which coincided with a national trend, did Busby prosper financially. But his good fortune soon slipped away when he invested heavily in a downward market. When he died he was nearly penniless, bankrupted by his own buildings.

CHAPTER ONE

EARLY LIFE AND CAREER 1786 - 1817

Born on 27 June 1786,(1) Charles Augustin Busby was one of seven children of whom five - two younger brothers and two sisters - survived their early years. As an almost completely self-taught man, their father, Dr Thomas Busby (1755-1838), saw no reason for his children to attend school; all were educated at home.

Dr Busby's professional interests were influential in forming Charles Augustin's career. He possessed the ability to earn his living by reporting parliamentary debates, playing the organ, composing music (his doctorate was in music),(2) writing poetry, teaching languages and singing, compiling musical dictionaries and translating from the Ancients. But it was Dr Busby's fascination with "mathematics, mechanics, perspective, optics, pneumatics and the philosophy of sound"(3) which especially engaged the attention of the young Charles, leading to his studies in architecture and engineering.

Dr Busby was also a Radical in politics, and never lost an opportunity of pleading the

1
A view of the London Dock, designed by D.A. Alexander, engraved and published by William Daniell, 1808. Busby worked on the Dock when a pupil in Alexander's office, acquiring the skills of architect and engineer.

Whig cause in the foreword of his books. Charles took up his father's politics. In his later life, Charles's strong liberal sympathies worked in his favour, as he found clients who were politically sympathetic.

The children's other tutor was their mother, formerly Miss Angier of Earl's Court, a woman of considerable knowledge combined with a fine sense of elegance that had been polished by her familiarity with the great families of Ireland.(4) First in their Poland Street house in Soho - where William Blake was a neighbour(5) - and afterwards in their China Terrace residence in Vauxhall, the Busby children received a precocious education. At 11 years of age, one of Charles's brothers was declared a musical prodigy. His other young brother, George Frederic - a namesake of Handel - had plunged into a complete translation from the Latin of the heroic poem *Thebais* by Statius.(6)

C.A. Busby commenced his pupillage with Daniel Asher Alexander (1768-1846) around 1802, his sixteenth year, the usual age to begin architectural training. Alexander's twin, and complementary, professions were to become Busby's. Just as Alexander called himself an "architect-engineer", so too did Busby.

When Busby joined Alexander's office, located in Laurence Pountney Lane in the City, Alexander was just beginning on one of his largest schemes, the London Docks, Wapping: a vast 20 acre site of warehouses, canals, locks and basin located east of the Tower, built to handle all ships, other than those arriving from the East and West Indies, carrying tobacco, rice, wine and brandy. (Fig.1) So immense was the project that it occupied Alexander's office for more than a quarter of a century.

Although only a young pupil, Busby's aptitude for absorbing technical detail enabled him to understand the two major complexities of the scheme. First, there was the hydraulic mechanics of the lock and canal system that allowed the laden cargo vessels to enter from the river into the peaceful haven of the inner docks. On this part of the project Busby would have rubbed shoulders with the leading canal and bridge engineer of the day, Thomas Telford, who acted in tandem with Alexander on the London Dock. Busby, fascinated by the effects of harnessing water, was later to take out patents for his own water lock and canal designs. Secondly, Busby was able to study Alexander's structural innovations. "Alexander's great forte," states Papworth's *Dictionary of Architecture*, "consists in original and novel ideas of construction";(7) a sentiment still expressed by today's engineering historians who consider the trussed roof of the New Tobacco Warehouse of the London Dock a brilliant experiment in iron construction.(8) Here again, was a case of where Alexander led, Busby followed; later in his career, Busby designed iron roofs which became the subject of considerable controversy.

There were many more projects being carried out in Alexander's office for Busby to cut his teeth on. Between 1805 and 1812, Alexander built Dartmoor Prison. In style and construction, Alexander borrowed from his warehouse architecture, using massive piers and vaults, and light iron roofs and columns.

Busby may also have worked on converting Inigo Jones's Queen's House in Greenwich for the Royal Naval Asylum for Children.(9) (Fig.2) Two long blocks of schoolrooms were added on either side and linked by Doric colonnades sensitively placed in relation to Wren's Royal Hospital near the River Thames. Such lessons in formal planning were not lost on Busby, who was to revive the Baroque approach of Wren and Alexander - employing an enclosed space fronting onto water - in his planning of Brighton and Hove.

Busby's training with Alexander was supplemented with an education available only to a selected number of aspiring young architects: evening classes at the Royal Academy Schools. The Schools gave Busby the opportunity to acquire a formal grounding in the classical vocabulary of architecture and to improve his drawing technique. Busby entered, upon Alexander's recommendation, as a probationer on 15 July 1803.(10) This allowed him student privileges of attending lectures, consulting the books in the library and drawing from the Schools' collection of architectural casts. His first exercises were for elementary schemes based on the antique, and included such projects as designing a Roman bath house.(11)

From 1801 to 1811, except for 1804, Busby had drawings selected annually to hang in the Royal Academy Exhibition.(12) During his early years, he mainly submitted designs for generic building types: in 1801, a mansion; in 1802, a park entrance; in 1803, a church, and two designs for a cathedral. In 1805, he exhibited a measured drawing of Worcester Cathedral, a work somewhat in the same vein, although undoubtedly more mature in technique, than his earliest surviving drawing, a part elevation of St Paul's Cathedral, dated November 1801.(13) Busby submitted an internal view of Westminster Abbey in 1806; and in the following year, two drawings for a Temple of Fame, of which only the plan has survived, showing a circular building ringed by 32 columns in the Roman style.(14)

In 1806, Busby entered the competition for a building in Croydon, Surrey, combining the

2
The Royal Naval Asylum, now the National Maritime Museum, Greenwich, by D. A. Alexander, 1807-10. A formal lesson in planning grand buildings near water which Busby later reapplied at Brighton and Hove.

unlikely union of law courts and butter market.(15) (Colour plate II) Although Busby's entry was unsuccessful, his design showed the strong influence of Alexander's warehouse architecture.(16) The market was set amongst the lower storeys of muscular brick arches while the two courtrooms, situated above, were each ceremoniously approached by staircases twisting around one another.

In July 1807, a few weeks after celebrating his twenty-first birthday, Busby and his brothers had their portraits painted by the miniaturist, J. Fruman.(17) (Colour plate I) The miniature of Busby shows him as a handsome, fresh-faced young man, fashionably dressed with a high shirt collar and black coat. His hands rest lightly clasping a large leather-bound volume, perhaps a copy of an architectural treatise, or more likely one of his father's many works.

Busby's student days at the Royal Academy were crowned by his winning the Gold Medal for his design for a building to house the Royal Academy, the Royal Society and the Society of Antiquaries. On 10 December 1807, in the presence of many of the Royal Academicians - including the painters J.M.W. Turner and Paul Sandby, the sculptor John Flaxman, and the architect John Soane - the long-standing President of the Royal Academy, Benjamin West handed Busby his medal.(18) West complimented Busby upon his design, to which Busby replied with a short speech. Joseph Farington - painter, gossip and diarist - who witnessed the event, was impressed by Busby's confidence.(19)

Enrolment in the architectural section of the Royal Academy Schools had been dropping steadily since 1798 when George Dance junior had taken up the post of Professor of Architecture, but had not fulfilled his obligation of delivering the six annual lectures.(20) Students wanted lectures and properly regulated discussions. Their frustration was increased by an inability to travel outside Britain, her colonies and the countries of her allies. The wars with France and America, and the rise and spread of the Napoleonic Empire, meant that for close on two decades many of the major monuments, buildings and sites on the Continent were inaccessible to Busby and his contemporaries.

In 1806 this situation led Busby and several of his fellow articled architects in Alexander's office who also attended the Schools, to found a group called the London Architectural Society.(21) Their President was Joseph Woods the younger (1776-1864); Busby acted as Secretary; and there were two Vice-Presidents, James Elmes (1782-1862) and James Savage (1779-1852).(22)

The Society's method was dialectic. Meeting every second Friday, from the last in October to the first in May, members were obliged to produce two projects annually: an essay on a subject related to civil architecture and an architectural design, not previously shown publicly, that had to be accompanied by critical and explanatory observations. Like Busby, most members were naturally interested in

3
Nightingale Cottage, Clapham, Surrey, built 1807. A plate from Busby's *Villas and Country Houses* (1808).

new technology, or "the science of architecture" as they called it. Many of their projects thus concentrated on engineering topics, especially bridge construction.

In 1808, Busby published one of his essays for the London Architectural Society as the introduction to his first pattern book, *A Series of Designs for Villas and Country Houses adapted with economy to the Comforts and to the Elegances of Modern Life with plans and explanations to each*. The publisher was Josiah Taylor, a fellow member, and proprietor of the Architectural Library in Holborn.

In both his essay and designs, Busby explored his interest in the picturesque and his taste for the Greek Revival. The essay begins with a brief history of architecture in which Busby praises "the science of Architecture" of the Italian Renaissance and condemns Robert Adam for "the adoption of the most trivial ornaments where strength and solidity should be the prominent characteristics." In reaction to Adam, Busby insisted that buildings be simple in their ornamentation, symmetrically planned, and take a subordinate place in the landscape. "The true impressions of cheerfulness, elegance, and refinement," he wrote optimistically, "are so well understood and so happily united in our modern domestic dwellings, that I hesitate not to say we are rapidly advancing to a state of perfection."(23)

Of the dozen designs in his publication, one had already been constructed during the spring of 1807 (Fig.3). This was for a villa in Nightingale Lane, near Clapham Common, Surrey, the first of at least three villas which Busby built in the Clapham area.(24) (Fig.4) In accordance with his preference for simplicity, Busby's villa was adaptable to living and entertainment. A central staircase created a theatrical impression, while rooms off the hall could be thrown open to form one large space for parties. Of Nightingale Cottage, Busby wrote with satisfaction, "it is a fact I am allowed to state, that the numerous accommodations

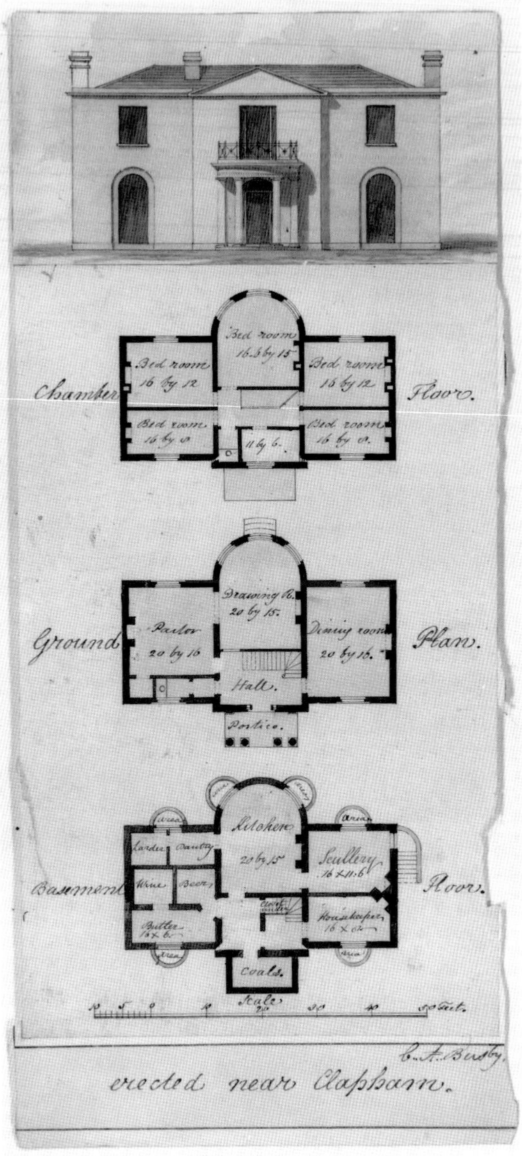

4
Design for a villa "erected near Clapham", c1808. One of a series of semi-rural villas by Busby on the outskirts of London.

5
Design, not executed, for Southampton Chapel, Fitzroy Square, London. Exhibited at the Royal Academy in 1808.

in this house have, on inspection, surprised most persons who judged of it only by its external appearance."(25)

Busby quickly followed his first volume with another, around 1810, which concentrated on decorative details. The title of the work fully summed up the nature of the contents: *A Collection of Designs for Modern Embellishments suitable to Parlours, Dining & Drawing Rooms, Folding Doors, Chimeny Pieces, Verandas, Frizes, etc. on 25 Plates*. With its hand-coloured plates, it was one of the prettiest pattern books produced during the Regency period. Busby advocated interiors decorated with pattern and colour: friezes of polka-dotted Greek key motifs on pink backgrounds; walls of elaborate plastered or painted decorative patterns of bright pink and blue, oriental fantasies intermingling with contemporary French designs on surfaces of cool yellows and greens. Doorways were to be heavily carved; the marble chimneypieces crowned by urns. Busby's finest achievements were his balcony designs of lattice-work, anthemions, antefixae and other wrought-iron delicacies. (See back cover) The pattern book served as a gentle advertisement for Busby's youthful talents.

In 1808, Busby exhibited at the Royal Academy a series of villa and country house designs from his publications, and a design for the Southampton Chapel, Fitzroy Square, Bloomsbury.(26) (Fig.5) The chapel design was probably one of his last student works; behind a symmetrical Greek front was an exceptional internal arrangement for a chapel of the Established Church, with the congregation seating facing towards the centre of the auditorium, focused on the pulpit and reading desk, not the altar.

Busby showed five different designs at the Royal Academy Exhibition of 1809. These were a mix of theoretical and practical, of student exercises and building works in progress. His Gold Medal design for a new Royal Academy hung beside those for a cathedral, a temple, one of his Clapham villas, and another villa which he had designed near Windsor, for S. Dixon.(27)

In 1809, Busby received his first important commission - the Commercial Coffee Rooms in Bristol. Busby had spotted the advertisement for the competition in a London newspaper in July 1809.(28) He entered and won in a field of seven other competitors. After London, Bristol boasted England's second largest port. The city's merchant class, wedded tightly to international commerce, was a large and fraternal society, always eager to compete with their brothers in London. The Bristol Rooms were considered a rival to the capital's famous meeting place, Lloyd's coffee house.(29)

Concerned that the Bristol committee might be taken aback by his youth and inexperience, because he was only 23, Busby turned to John Soane for a reference. Soane replied, "I have seen several of your works and shall be happy to bear testimony to their merit."(30) In the end, the reference was not required but Busby, delighted, wrote back to Soane to express how it would "always be a source of the proudest satisfaction to have met with the appreciation of a Gentleman who had attained the first eminence of his profession."(31)

Within a week of winning, Busby was in Bristol discussing changes to his design with the building committee. The stone façade of his Greek temple, with its Ionic portico, was to remain unaltered. (Fig.6) But the committee of Bristol found the interior decoration too ornate, and asked Busby to pare some away. As compensation, the lantern, over the principal room was to be made a feature by extending it to a diameter of 14 feet. And instead of pilasters, 12 caryatids were inserted between the circle of windows at the base of the lantern (Colour plate III); this was Busby's homage to the Three-Percent Room of the Bank of England, where a decade earlier Soane too had spun a circle of caryatids beneath a dome.

Busby asked his friend and colleague from the Royal Academy Schools and the London Architectural Society, James George Bubb (1782-1853), to execute the three sculptural figures that grace the Corn Street front. At the apex of the pediment is the figure of the City of Bristol, shield and trident in hand. To either side are the figures of Commerce, who holds a caduceus, and Navigation - both potent symbols for the building's patrons. Bubb also sculpted the very fine, 17 foot long basso relief within the portico showing Britannia, attended

6
The Corn Street front of the Commercial Coffee Rooms, Bristol. Busby's first major commission, built 1809-11.

by Neptune and Minerva, receiving tributes from the four quarters of the globe.

Busby attended the impressive ceremony of laying the foundation stone on 19 March 1810. He walked in the procession, from the Council House to the flag-bedecked building site, behind the Clerk of the Works who held the building plans, and in front of the Mayor and his mace-bearer. The crowds turned out in great number to watch. Afterwards, a celebratory dinner was held during which, while dessert was being served, a poem written especially for the event by Dr Busby was distributed and read. Great applause greeted the heroic couplet:

> A structure rises, founded by her zeal,
> Sacred to commerce and the public
> weal. (32)

The jubilant mood was not to last. A year after the project began, the building committee again started to fuss over the costs of the internal decoration and decided to make a comparative inspection of similar establishments. The chairman of the group, George Dyer, and the committee secretary visited the Exchange and the Portico Library in Manchester, and the Exchange and the Athenaeum Lyceum in Liverpool. As a result, Busby received a stiff letter in which the committee pointed out that "we have only to lament that the Journey had not been taken much sooner than it was."(33) The committee's greatest regret was the cost of the five white ornamental chimney pieces which Bubb was executing. The black ones they had seen on their visits looked fine and cost only half the price. Bubb, quite naturally, refused to give up his commission, although in the end not all five were delivered and black marble fireplaces predominate.

7
Unexecuted design for an apollonicon for the Commercial Coffee Rooms, Bristol, 1814. This giant organ, 30 feet high, could be played by six musicians.

The affair over the expense of the decoration did not mar Busby's relations with the committee. In February 1811 he designed a lunette decoration of nereids presenting the Bristol coat-of-arms, which Bubb was to sculpt.(34) But this came to nothing.

The Commercial Coffee Rooms opened in October 1811. Beneath the gaze of the caryatids, and lit by the Grecian lampshades made by a local glass-maker Isaac Jacobs, Bristol merchants were able to drink coffee and exchange business news, just as they do today.

A few years after the completion of the Commercial Rooms, Busby was asked back by the committee. To celebrate the conclusion of the Napoleonic War at the end of 1814, the Rooms had been specially illuminated.(35) It was probably for just such a jubilant occasion that the committee commissioned Busby to design a commemorative work - an apollonicon, (Fig.7) a great chamber organ which mechanically produced the sound of the entire orchestra, and had been invented two years before by the organ builders Flight and Robson. Dr Busby, in his book *Concert Room and Orchestra Anecdotes of Music and Musicians, Ancient and Modern* (1825), illustrated and enthusiastically described this contrivance on which six musicians, each playing upon their own keyboard, "develop the various powers of the organic construction, and operate on the nerves and feelings of the auditors in a truly surprising manner."(36)

The apollonicon set up by Flight and Robson in their St Martin's Lane shop was a plain affair compared with Busby's fantasy.(37) If it had been built, Busby's instrument would have reached 30 feet into the air. With its four pilasters topped by lyre capitals, and its sculpture of Apollo, the god of music, it resembled nothing less than a pagan altar. But, unfortunately, this was another of Busby's projects that failed to materialize.

The success of the Bristol Commercial Rooms enabled Busby, in 1810, to move from his parent's home at 36 Queen Anne Street, near Oxford Street, London, where the family had lived since 1805, to a house in Warwick Court, Gray's Inn. The following year he moved once again, to 4 Hart Street, Bloomsbury.

Busby now turned to a series of commissions for country villas. One of these was for Serge Hill House, near Abbots Langley in

8
The entrance and garden fronts of Serge Hill House, near Abbots Langley, Hertfordshire. Busby designed this country villa in 1811.

9
The lantern over the staircase, Serge Hill House.

10
The staircase, Serge Hill House.

Hertfordshire, for which he exhibited designs at the Royal Academy in 1811.(38) The house is a simple, two storey brick structure, the only external features being the Doric portico and the double-height bow front to take advantage of the beautiful views across the countryside. (Fig.8) Busby gave the internal staircase a spectacular flourish: its soaring flight being top-lit by a cupola with glazed sides and a rosette. (Figs.9 & 10)

An even grander scheme, but one not built, was a country house Busby designed for John Thomas Wasey, a solicitor and land speculator from Newbury, Berkshire.(39) The house, with its plan dominated again by a great staircase, was to have been approached up a sweeping drive.(40)

Meanwhile, Busby was busy working on his entries for two competitions. One was for new assembly rooms at Leamington Spa, which had been advertised in February 1811.(41) Fresh from his Bristol triumph, he tried his hand at creating another club-like atmosphere.(42) In this case he renounced the classical temple in favour of a plain treatment. (Fig.11) Entry was to be either by the central doors into the coffee and reading room, or through the loggia leading to another of Busby's top-lit staircases, this one decorated with niches for lamps and sculpture. On the first floor, visitors would have passed through an ante-room into the ballroom - a hall 30 feet high - from which after the pleasure of the dance they could retire to the refreshment or card rooms. But the commission for the Leamington Spa Assembly Rooms went to Charles

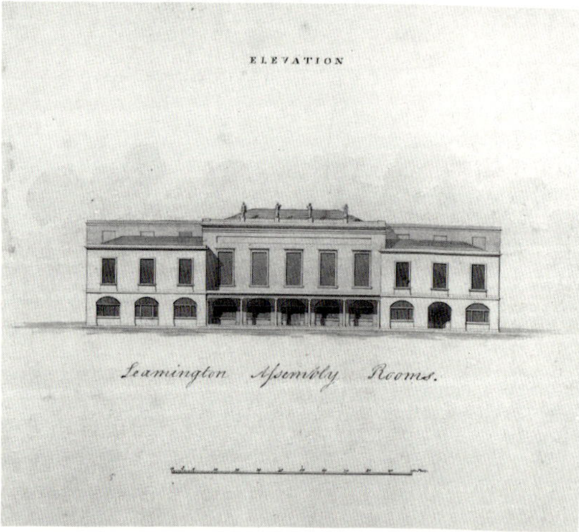

11
Unexecuted competition design for the Assembly Rooms, Royal Leamington Spa, *c*1811.

12
Half-plan for a penitentiary for 612 convicts, *c*1815. The missing right half of the drawing would have mirrored the surviving fragment.

Smith, who had been one of Busby's fellow students at the Royal Academy.

Success also eluded Busby in the next competition he entered, although he did gain second place, an honorary premium of £100, and a good degree of recognition.(43) The contest was for the new Millbank Penitentiary, to be sited on the marshy banks of the Thames south of the Palace of Westminster. It was to be Europe's largest prison, built to house the convict population of London.

The guiding light behind Millbank had been George Holford M.P., responsible in 1812 for choosing John Williams's winning design from amongst the 43 entries.(44) Holford, like many of his contemporaries interested in the reform of the penal system, held strong views about prison design. Two particular events had spurred this interest. The first had been the investigations made by John Howard in the 1770s and '80s into the deplorable state of British prisons. The second, in response to this growing movement to improve the health and welfare of the prisoner, was Jeremy Bentham's development around 1790 of a theoretical prison design, which he called the Panopticon, that placed prison cells in a radiating fashion around a central block.(45) Architects and reformers alike were soon debating the wisdom of Bentham's radial plan as opposed to the polygonal plan in which cellblocks were arranged in clusters.

Holford favoured the polygonal plan.(46) It is therefore most likely that Busby's entry - which has not survived - followed this pattern and was very similar to his sketch design, that does exist, for a penitentiary to house 612 inmates.(47) (Fig.12) At the nucleus of the surviving design, Busby inserted the governor's house and the chapel: the centres of temporal and spiritual authority in the

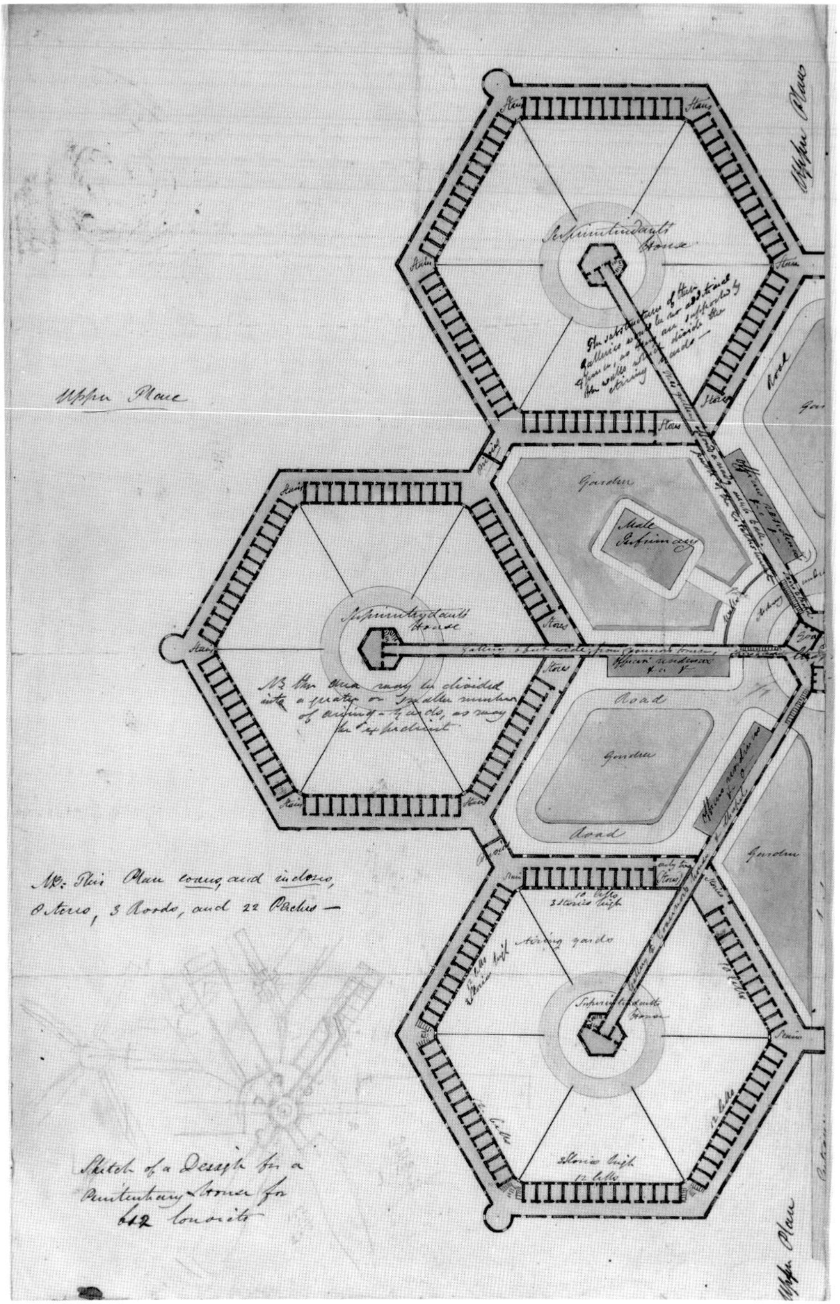

prisoner's life. Pivoting in an orbital ring around these were to be six autonomous six-sided blocks, each containing 102 cells. At the heart of each of these blocks was a large open court with a superintendent's house and an inspection tower that was in turn linked by a long secure corridor to the governor's house and chapel. In fact, Busby's design shows remarkable similarities to Millbank as it was completed by Robert Smirke.(48)

Busby, however, was not wedded to the polygonal plan. Having worked with Alexander on Dartmoor Prison, and perhaps on Maidstone County Goal - begun in 1810 on a radial plan - Busby's experimental nature led him to design a variety of penitentiary plans. In the bottom corner of his polygonal prison drawing he roughly sketched several radial plans showing cell blocks dispersed from a central block, rather like the spokes of a wheel. These sketches were his preliminary ideas for one of the two designs he submitted in May 1816 to the Corporation of Bristol when they were seeking plans for a new gaol on the site of the Castle Green.(49) (Fig.13)

But undoubtedly the most inventive of his

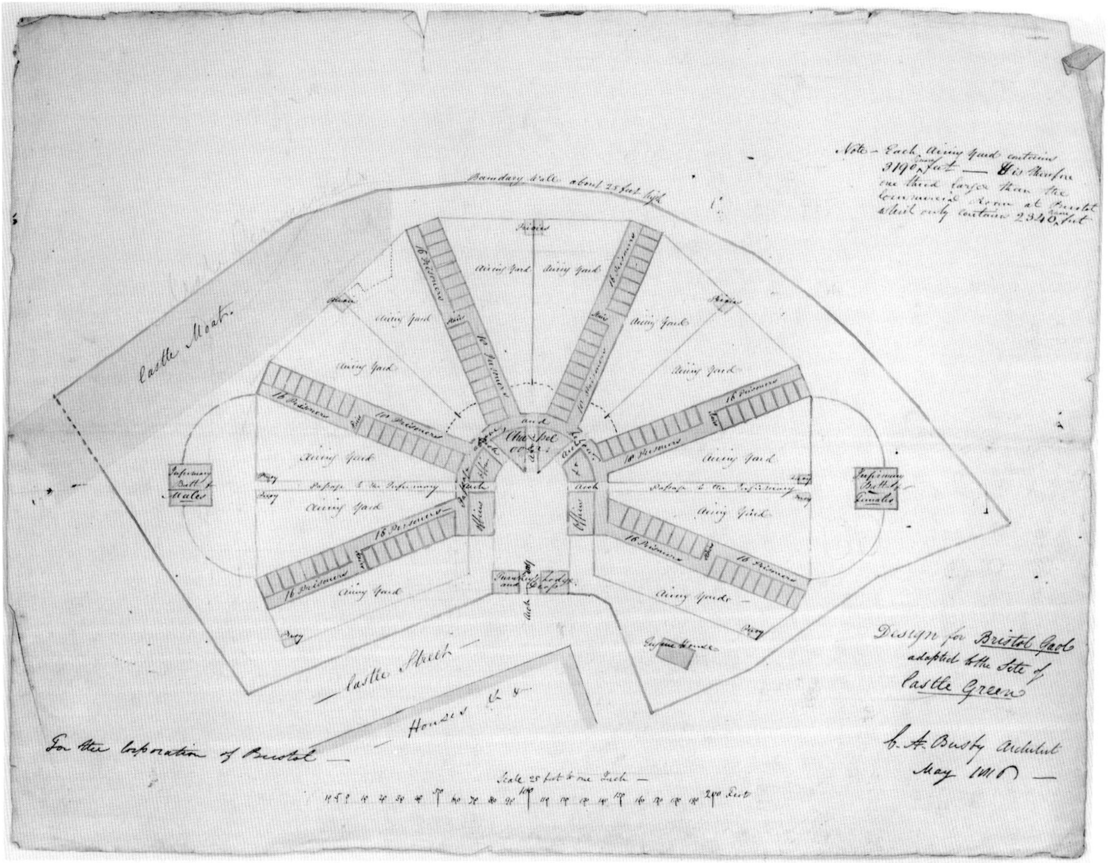

13
Radial plan design, not executed, for Bristol Goal, 1816. Busby's interest in prison design was a reflection of his strong social conscience.

Bristol plans was the one in the shape of a heart.(50) (Fig.14) Prisoners, probably unappreciative of the irony of the layout, would have dwelt in cells overlooking a central courtyard and, in turn, be overlooked by turnkeys and supervisors in central towers. The two sections which Busby drew at the top and bottom of the sheet show the grim reality from which the felons of Bristol were spared; none of Busby's schemes were built.

In 1813, Busby joined with a former fellow student from the Royal Academy Schools, George Maliphant, to design and build a chapel and schools in London's East End. The London Society for Promoting Christianity Amongst the Jews was an evangelical movement created to do exactly as its name suggested, convert Jews. Busby and Maliphant erected the Society's headquarters in Palestine Place just off Cambridge Heath Road in Bethnal Green. (Fig.15) This was the chapel where in the late 1830s the young George Gilbert Scott attended services amongst a congregation of "New Lights".(51) The architects chose a simple solution. The chapel, a plain Greek Revival affair, was placed at the centre of two utilitarian

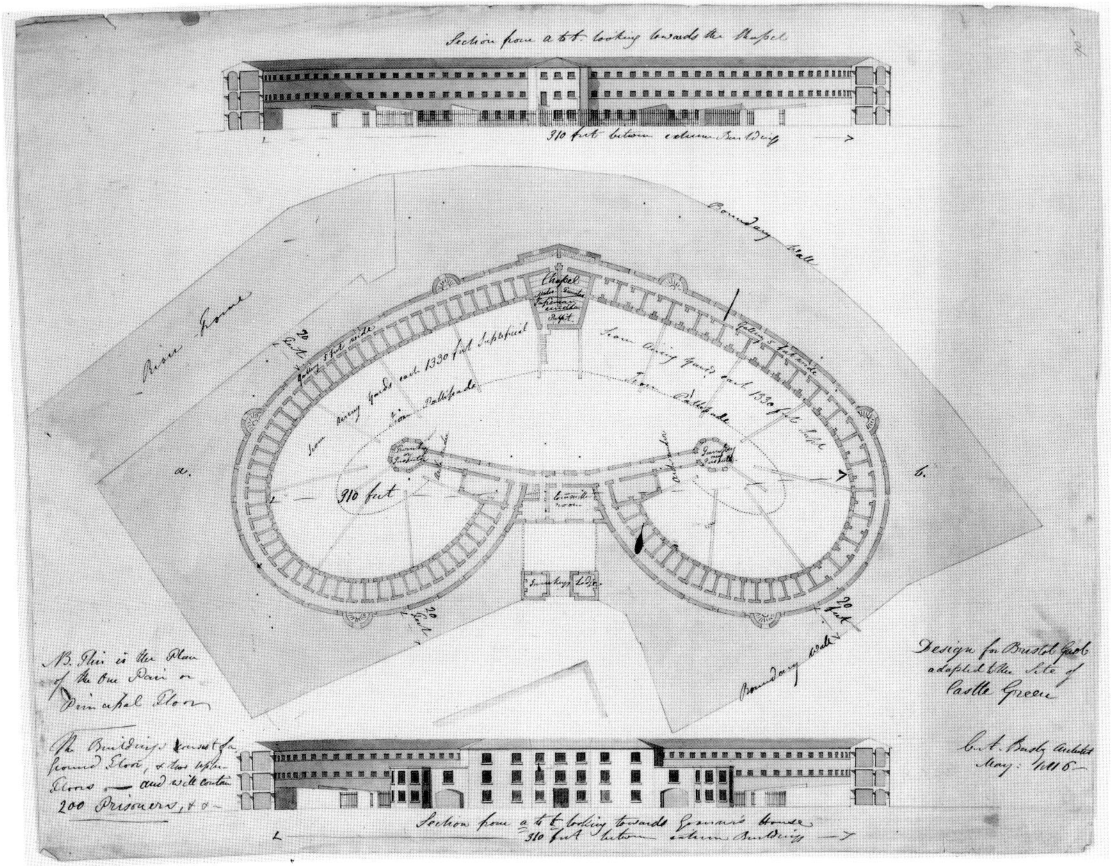

14
Heart shaped plan design, not executed, for Bristol Goal, 1816.

15
The chapel and schools of the London Society for Promoting Christianity Amongst the Jews, Cambridge Heath Road, Bethnal Green, London. Designed by Busby and George Maliphant (now demolished). This print is contemporary with the building's construction, *c*1813.

PERSPECTIVE VIEW

OF THE

Chapel, Schools, &c.

INTENDED TO BE ERECTED

BY THE

London Society,

FOR PROMOTING

Christianity amongst the Jews.

buildings that housed schoolrooms and offices.(52)

The foundation stone for the Jews' Chapel was laid on 7 April 1813. The following year Busby and Maliphant exhibited a view of their scheme at the Royal Academy.(53)

It was during this period that Busby began his experiments in hydraulic engineering. In November 1812, he submitted a complicated but innovative scheme for a lock system to operate on the Regent's Canal. The project to run a canal along the northern boundary of the fledgling Regent's Park had been backed the previous year by the Park's designer, John Nash. The chief engineer for the Regent's Canal was James Morgan, who with little knowledge of canal construction had experienced difficulty in overcoming the crucial need to save as much water as possible when locks were used, thus making fresh supplies unnecessary.

Busby claimed he had all but solved the problem: "I therefore proceed to state, that I have discovered an entirely new, and efficacious means of elevating and depressing the surfaces of the water contained between the gates of common Canal Locks, to a height, or depth, equal to the interval between the upper and lower levels of the water contiguous to those locks, more rapidly than in the usual manner, and with a very small loss of water."(54) The Canal Committee were invited to Busby's new premises at 12 Millman Street in Gray's Inn to see a large working model of the invention.(55) At one point in the discussions, Busby met Nash and the canal builder Charles, third Earl Stanhope, to demonstrate his invention.(56)

But though Busby refined his locking system and in 1813 took out a patent,(57) (Colour plate IV) it was not adopted for the Regent's Canal.

In early 1814, Busby began work on two commissions: one he took out of the hands of another architect, the other was to be taken out of his.

In 1811, the banker Henry Baring purchased Somerley, a large Hampshire country house designed during the 1790s by Samuel Wyatt.(58) Two years later, Baring commissioned the renowned landscape designer Humphry Repton and his son John Adey Repton to design an aviary in the form of a festive rustic temple.(59) But the following year, Baring asked Busby to re-work the scheme. (Colour plate V) Busby replaced Repton's aviary with a polygonal conservatory and keeper's cottage, and created a trellised walk constructed of delicate iron arches topped by anthemions and set on cast iron columns.(60)

At the same time as he was working on Somerley, Busby was also designing a large gothic castle. His patron was Lloyd Bamford Hesketh, a prominent landowner in North Wales. Hesketh was himself an amateur architect, and took a leading role in the design of Gwyrch Castle.

The setting for what has been described as "one of the most amazing 19th century castellated mansions, and one which the age in which it was conceived would have assigned to the realm of the sublime rather than the picturesque",(61) is high upon a rocky promontory above Abergele, overlooking the Irish Sea. For the first time in his career, Busby abandoned any notion of symmetrical planning to create this battlemented fantasy.(62) (Colour plate VI)

At first, Hesketh approved of Busby's scheme, and produced his own sketch the following year, in December 1815, which in all but minor details was a faithful reproduction of Busby's original.(63)

This was then followed by Busby's second scheme in May 1816, which incorporated several of Hesketh's suggestions to give the medieval character of the castle greater emphasis; the windows, for example, were gothicised.(64) But Hesketh, sensing perhaps that Busby was not well enough versed in the gothic language of architecture turned to an architect who was, Thomas Rickman. At first, Rickman worked up detailed designs for four cast-iron gothic windows for Gwyrch Castle. Impressed, Hesketh sent on Busby's drawings for Rickman's comments. "The General aspect I like," he replied. But Rickman had several criticisms, including the fact that the servants would have to walk through the best rooms because there were no service corridors or stairs. The architectural solecisms particularly irked Rickman's scholarly eye: "I observe that Mr Busby has put sills under all his Windows this is so very great a violation of propriety I cannot pass it with out notice none of our good works whether Ecclesiastical domestic or castellated has such a thing but a slope as I

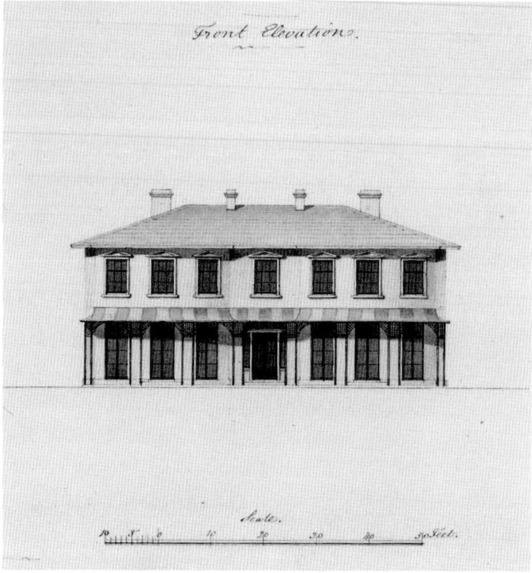

16
Unexecuted design for a house for Charles Clifton, Ty Mawr, Wales, 1815.

have shown in my windows with sometimes indeed a running Tablet under it but nothing like a Sill."(65) Hesketh appointed Rickman his architect.

By the time Rickman sent his own set of drawings based on Busby's design for Gwyrch, Busby had left the country. Hesketh was later to tinker with Rickman's advice so that the resulting castle, which began to be constructed in 1819, may be said to be Busby's in concept, and Rickman's and Hesketh's in detail.

While working on Gwyrch Castle, Busby was designing several other residences, very different in scale and conception. One was also in Wales, for Charles Claude Clifton, who inhabited the ancient mansion of Ty Maur, a fortified farmhouse in the village of Llanfrynach, some three miles southeast of Brecon. Busby had the drawings ready for Clifton's inspection in March 1815.(66) (Fig.16) With its pretty striped awnings and tall windows onto the garden, had Clifton decided to build to Busby's designs, he would have found himself living in the style of a Regency gentleman instead of that of a country squire.

In December 1815, Busby prepared two variant house designs for Mrs Powys Floyd of Sidmouth, Devon, a fashionable Regency seaside resort already boasting several houses in the picturesque style.(67) (Figs.17 & 18) Powys Cottage, long and thatched, was to be one of the grandest in town. Both of Busby's designs were based on the same plan: a single storey divided by a 120 foot central passage with the private apartments aligned along the front and with the services to the rear. One of the designs had pointed windows under hood moulds, the other had rectangular windows with a projecting verandah. At the centre of the south front lay a conservatory room with a bay front, a warm and sunny place to sit and view the sea.(68)

The completed Powys Cottage, as recorded in several contemporary prints, was closest in detail to the non-gothic design.(69) Unfortunately, during the early 1870s an additional storey was added to the cottage, submerging Busby's elongated plan.

All in all, Busby's practice was not developing as rapidly as he wished. Finances were extremely tight. He began to circulate notices of his abilities, especially that of making models under a "new and perspicacious method of *substantial representation*" to facilitate more accurate estimates of a building's cost.(70)

And then disaster struck - the roof of one of his buildings collapsed. It is unrecorded which building failed, but the cause is known: a weakness due to one of Busby's experiments.(71) A surviving drawing by Busby for a curious wrought iron roof structure

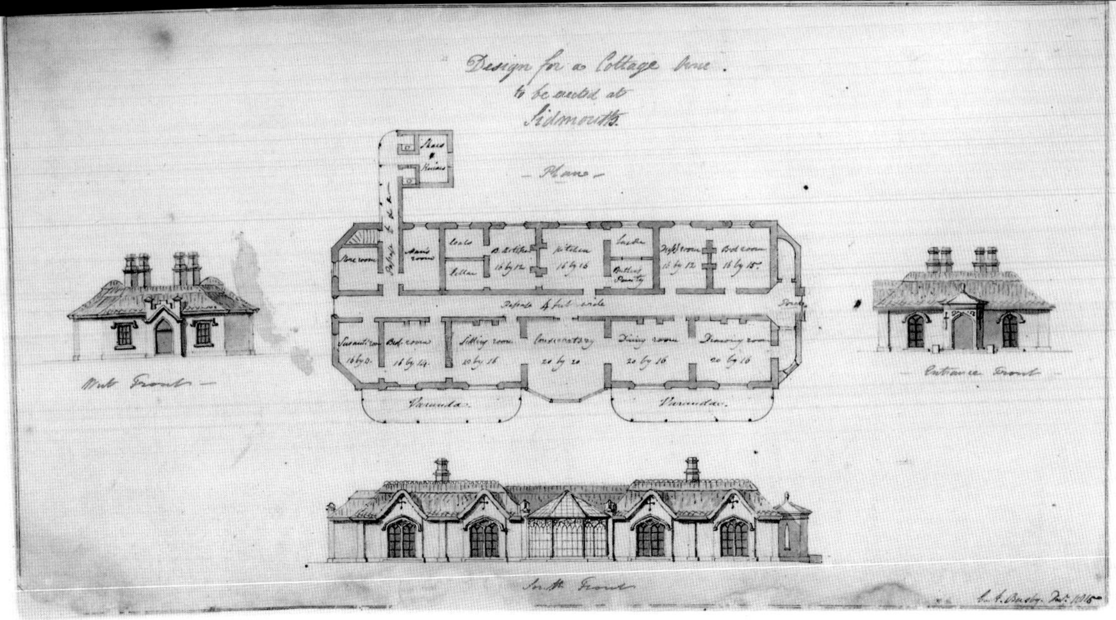

17
Gothic design for Powys Cottage, Sidmouth, Devon, 1815.

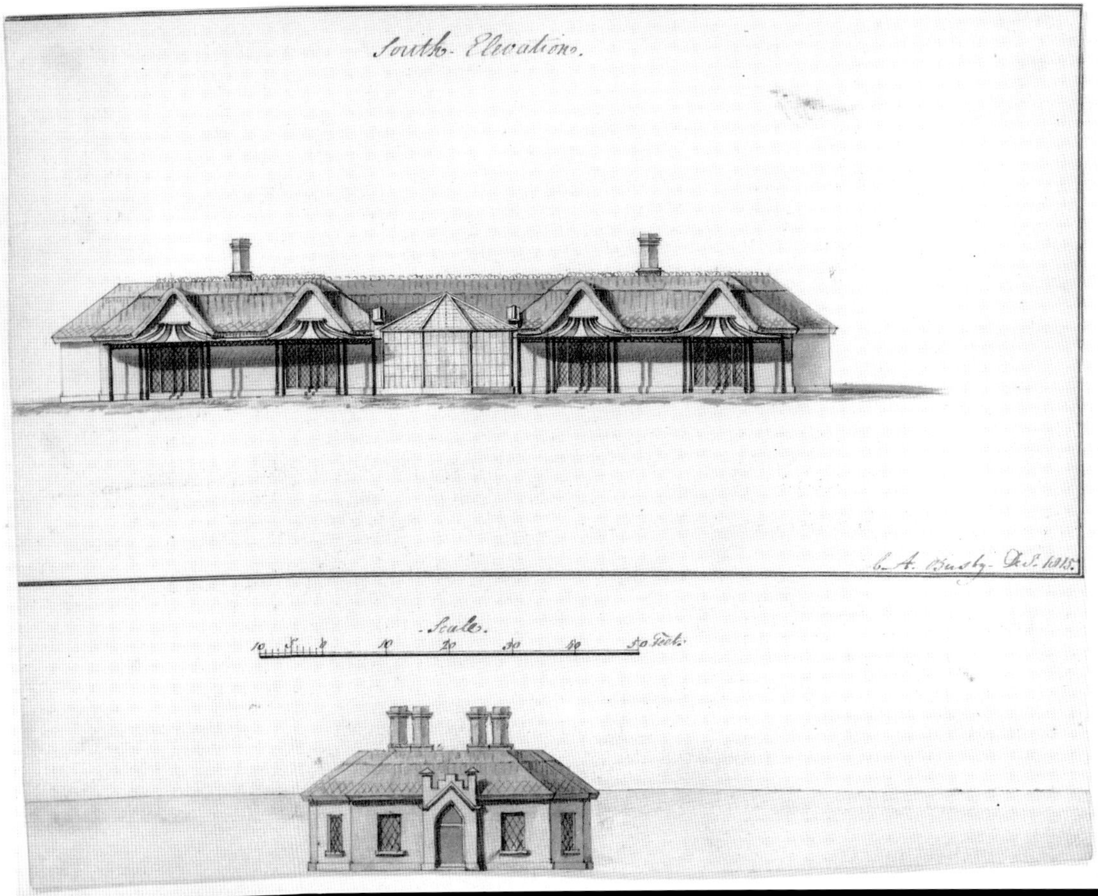

18
Canopy design for Powys Cottage, Sidmouth, Devon, 1815. An alternative exterior for Mrs Powys which still retained the central conservatory.

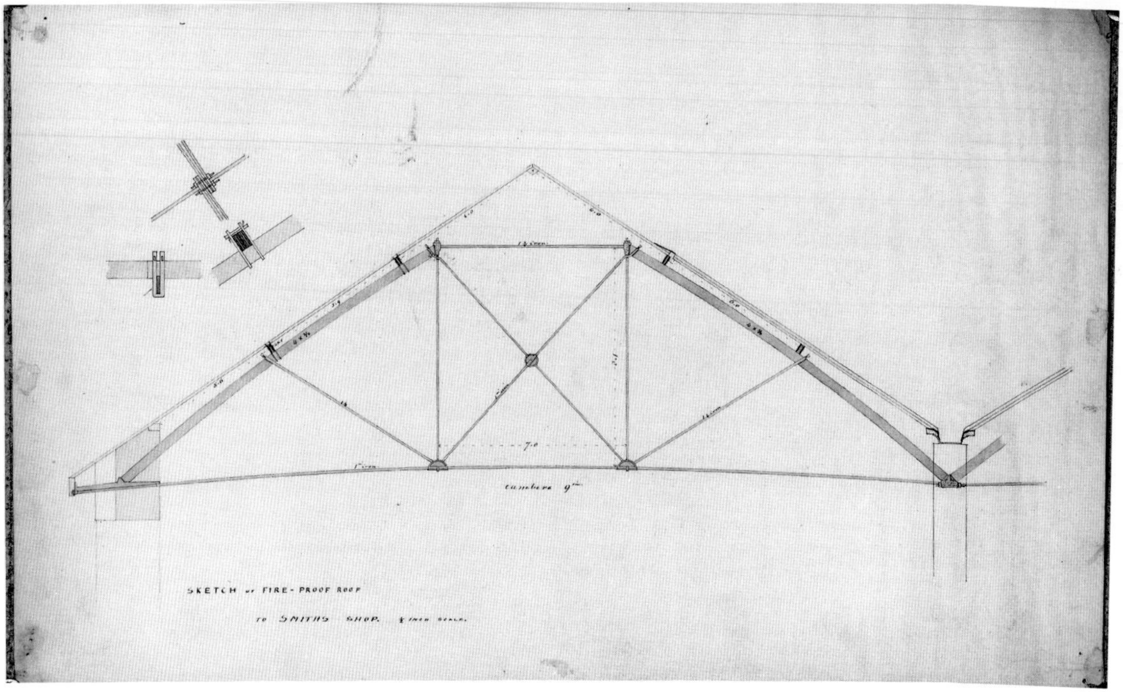

19
Design for an iron roof structure. This experimental truss may be of the type which collapsed, precipitating Busby's departure to America in 1817.

may well be the suspect work. (Fig.19) It is labelled "Sketch of fireproofed roof to Smiths Shop". The truss is most unconventional. The principal rafters do not meet at the apex, but instead are joined by central struts only one and a quarter inches thick. A modern structural analysis has revealed that, based on a number of assumptions, although the roof could cover a space of seven to ten feet, it is highly unstable.(72)

To add to his worries was the need to support a growing family. Busby had married Louisa Mary Williams on 3 July 1811.(73) Their first child, a son, had been born in April 1814, shortly after they had moved to 33 Berners Street in Soho. He was christened Charles Stanhope Burke Busby,(74) a combination of names which summed up his father's artistic and political aspirations: Charles, from Charles, Earl of Stanhope, the canal builder Busby had met on the Regent's Canal project, who was a radical with French revolutionary sympathies; and Burke, a reference to Edmund Burke, statesman and philosophical author on aesthetic theory.

Their second child, a daughter born 20 April 1817, was more simply named Ellen Mary Busby. Like her brother, she too was christened at the Church of St Marylebone.(75)

A few weeks after the ceremony for his daughter, C.A. Busby sailed for America - a classic case of a man setting out to seek his fortune.

CHAPTER TWO

IN AMERICA 1817 - 1819

Busby's first sight of the United States of America left him with a magical impression of the country's youthful confidence illustrated by its newest technology: "The Brooklyn steam-ferry-boat was the first moving object that arrested my attention as I entered the port of New-York. The effect, to me who had never witnessed the spontaneous march of the huge fabric, laden with carriages, horses, and men, now gliding past our ship, was delightful; and impressed upon my imagination a more elevated idea of the enterprising spirit of the New World, than would the most lofty panegyric, unaccompanied by the test before me."(1)

Steamboats were a novelty. They had been plying the Hudson River in regular service only since 1810 and were an almost exclusively American phenomenon. Busby, with his interest in hydraulic engineering, was eager to learn more about them.

In 1817, New York City was not America's leading or largest centre, but it was certainly one of the most thriving, well on its way to overtaking the larger cities of Philadelphia, Baltimore and Boston. On Manhattan, civilization was still mainly concentrated at the southern tip of the island, with a population of around 120,000. It was here that Busby lived for more than two years, for his first few months at 8 Wall Street, and then at 2 Law Buildings on Nassau Street.(2)

But his spiritual American home was a few blocks away, on Chambers Street, at the New-York Institution. Occupying an old almshouse, the Institution was the heart of the city's artistic, scientific and intellectual life, acting as the home to the New-York Historical Society, the American Academy of Fine Arts, the Lyceum of Natural History, the Literary and Philosophical Society and John Scudder's American Museum.(3)

Busby plunged into the Institution's affairs. At the first meeting of the New-York Historical Society that Busby attended on 10 June 1817, he was elected an Honorary Member.(4) The following month, on 5 July, he was proposed as an Associate Member of the American Academy.(5) And in September, the President of the Literary and Philosopical Society, the eminent physician Dr David Hosack, put forward Busby's name for membership.(6) As a new arrival, Busby had immediately been drawn into the town's highest circle.

His introduction had been made through one of the Institution's leading figures, Colonel John Trumbull (1756-1843), the famous patriot-artist of the American Revolution. Before embarking for the States, Busby had obtained a letter of introduction to Trumbull from the Pennsylvanian-born President of the Royal Academy, Benjamin West.(7) Trumbull took Busby under his wing during his American stay, and helped the young Englishman to make new friends.

The peace of 1815 between the United States and Great Britain had allowed Trumbull to return to his native America after more than 35 years in Europe. During many of these years he had studied and worked under West and then painted independently. He, like Busby, also had a strong political nature.(8)

Although the American Academy of Fine Arts had been founded in 1802, it was not until Trumbull joined in 1816 that the Academy was put on a proper footing. Trumbull's express aim was to model this American body on the Royal Academy in London. To this end, the American Academy began to hold annual exhibitions and elect Academicians and Associates. Busby became the Academy's architectural adviser.

Busby brought with him a selection of many of his best drawings and designs. At the first of the two American Academy exhibitions held in 1817, he showed the elevation and section of his Gold Medal drawings for a building to house the Royal Academy, the Royal Society and the Society of Antiquaries.(9) Impressed, Trumbull and members of the other societies directed Busby in August 1817 to prepare designs "for the improvement and embellishment" of the north and south fronts of the Institution building.(10) This was a larger task than the simple one of diverting the Institution's flues which Busby had undertaken the previous month.(11)

For the new works, $7500 was estimated. The Institution intended to apply to the State Legislature in the next session for financial assistance. With De Witt Clinton, mayor of the City of New York and Governor of the State, as the very active President of the Historical Society, the chances of government support seemed assured. Yet nothing ever came of the project.

As Busby awaited the funds, he sought other commissions. One of his first enterprises was to make a series of drawings of the buildings of New York. These were engraved by W. Hooke as illustrations to a guidebook, *Blunt's Stranger's Guide to the City of New York* (1817). Busby provided the only three vignettes in the guide: the front of the City Hall (New York's most exuberant building to date, by John McComb Jnr, opened in 1812), a cupola-capped almshouse, and the State Prison.

His next project, which proved unsuccessful, was undertaken as a labour of devotion and thanks. In July he hastened to Philadelphia, a city of established culture and much fine architecture. Busby's object was to look at a small building which had been recently constructed in the grounds of the Pennsylvania Hospital - the Picture House.

The one large picture which was to occupy this building had yet to leave England, *Christ Healing the Sick in the Temple* by Benjamin West. The Pennsylvania Hospital had asked West for the gift of a painting to help raise funds "for the relief of maniacs and sick poor", to which the artist readily agreed, wishing to assist one of the oldest and most important hospitals in his native country. The promised work, more than 16 feet long and 10 feet high, was completed in 1811, but proved to be such a success in London that West was obliged to paint another version for Philadelphia.(12)

West had expressed his disquiet to Busby about the building which was to receive his work: a castellated structure with pointed windows by a local builder named Webb. The President of the Hospital, Samuel Coates, had already received West's strong views in a passionate letter: "It is the *Gothic taste* I combat with, as inapplicable to the building in ques-

20
Busby's measured drawing of the Picture House, Pennsylvania Hospital, Philadelphia, 1817. Benjamin West objected to the "Gothic taste" for this building housing his painting *Christ Healing the Sick*.

tion, for that architecture is the insignia of a period, which the civilized world had passed away, science had fled, and the mind of man lay in darkness. Then arose mankinds superstition and mankinds taste - but now, that science has arisen, let the cities of America in their streets and highways proclaim its ascendancy by every visible mark of its eternal truth."(13)

In other words, West wanted a classical gallery. Busby tried to oblige. First he made a measured drawing of the elevation of the gothic building,(14) (Fig.20) and then he classicized it(15) (Fig.21) removing the crenellation and rounding the pointed windows. Busby probably sent a copy of his remodelled Picture House to West. The hospital committee, however, having spent $13,749.25

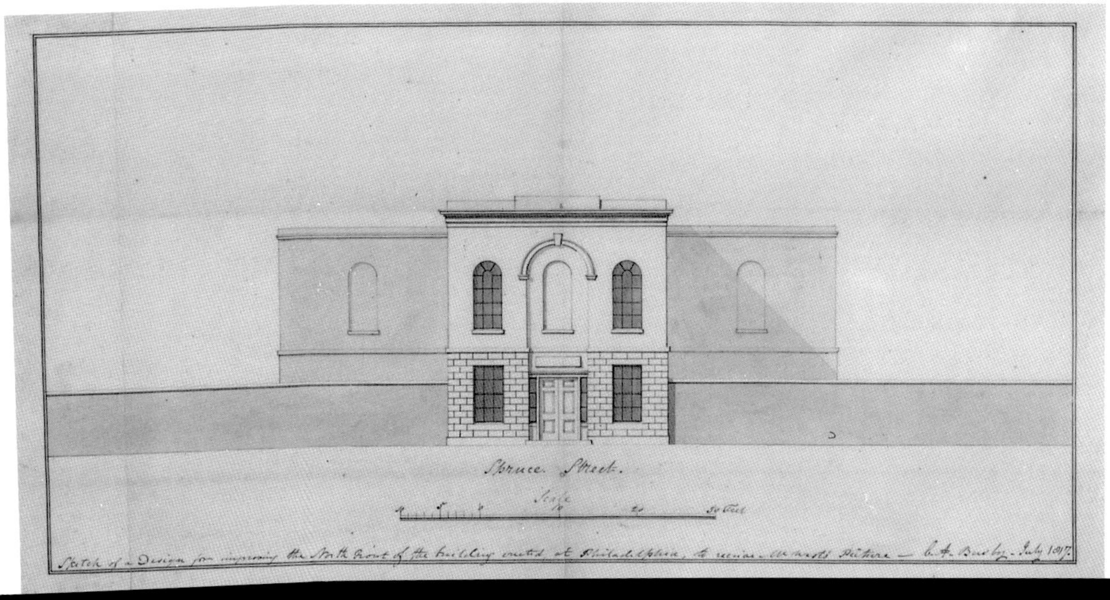

21
Classical design, not executed, for the Picture house, Pennsylvania Hospital, Philadelphia, 1817. Busby's reworking of the objectionable gothic building.

22
Elevation of the Bollingbrook Theatre, Petersburg, Virginia, 1817. Busby's only American building survived for more than a century.

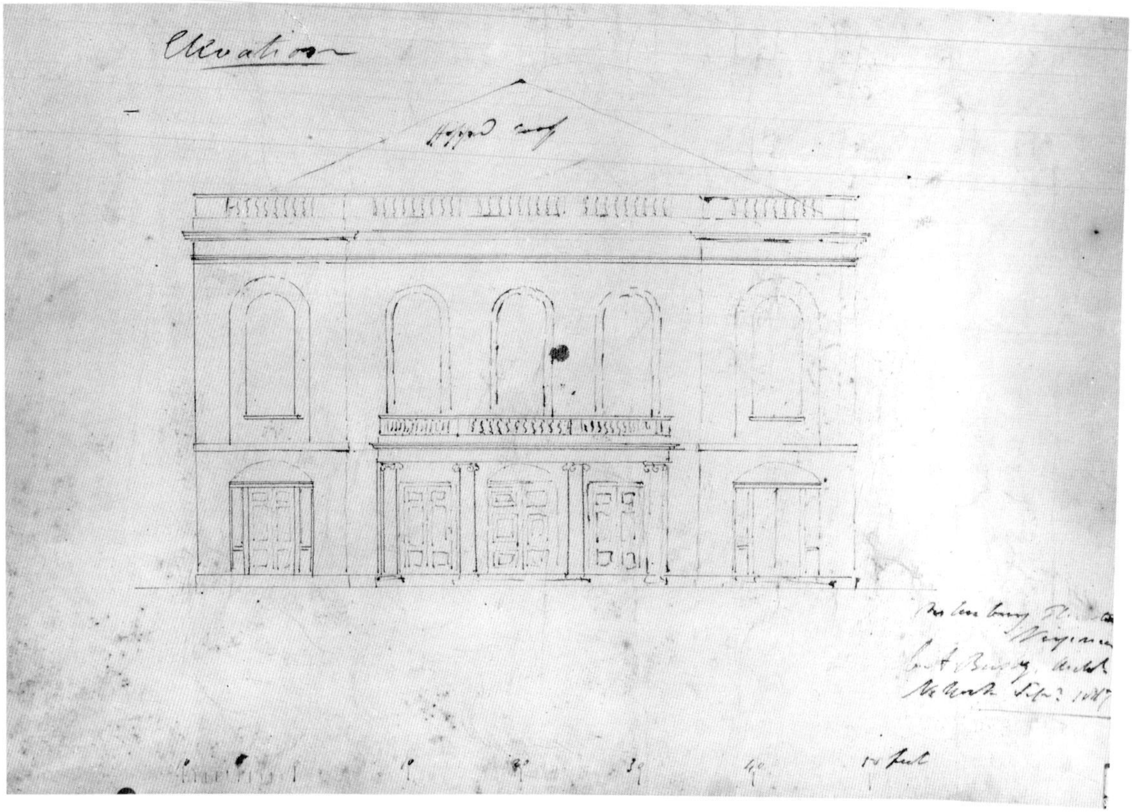

on the structure was not in the mood for a change.(16)

In September, Busby received a major architectural commission, for the Bollingbrook Theatre in Petersburg, Virginia. Time must have been short, for he hastily produced a rough set of drawings on thin paper without the aid of a ruler, a contrast to his usual meticulous draughtsmanship.(17) (Figs.22 & 23) In elevation, the theatre resembled his earlier design for Southampton Chapel. The principal entrance to the theatre was through three doors, beneath a semicircular Ionic portico, leading into the main vestibule. Ringing the auditorium, the three tiers of balconies and boxes were supported by iron columns - a very early use of structural iron in America.

Busby's theatre opened in 1818 and must have been a lavish affair for the town, costing about $20,000, the money having been raised on subscription by an English comedian and manager, James H. Caldwell.(18)

The thrill of his first sighting of an American steamboat had aroused Busby's spirit of invention. In June 1818 he published his latest findings in the *American Monthly Magazine*, an article he later expanded and published on its own. In this essay he wrote:

"Thus forcibly impressed, before I had even touched the American shores, and habitual

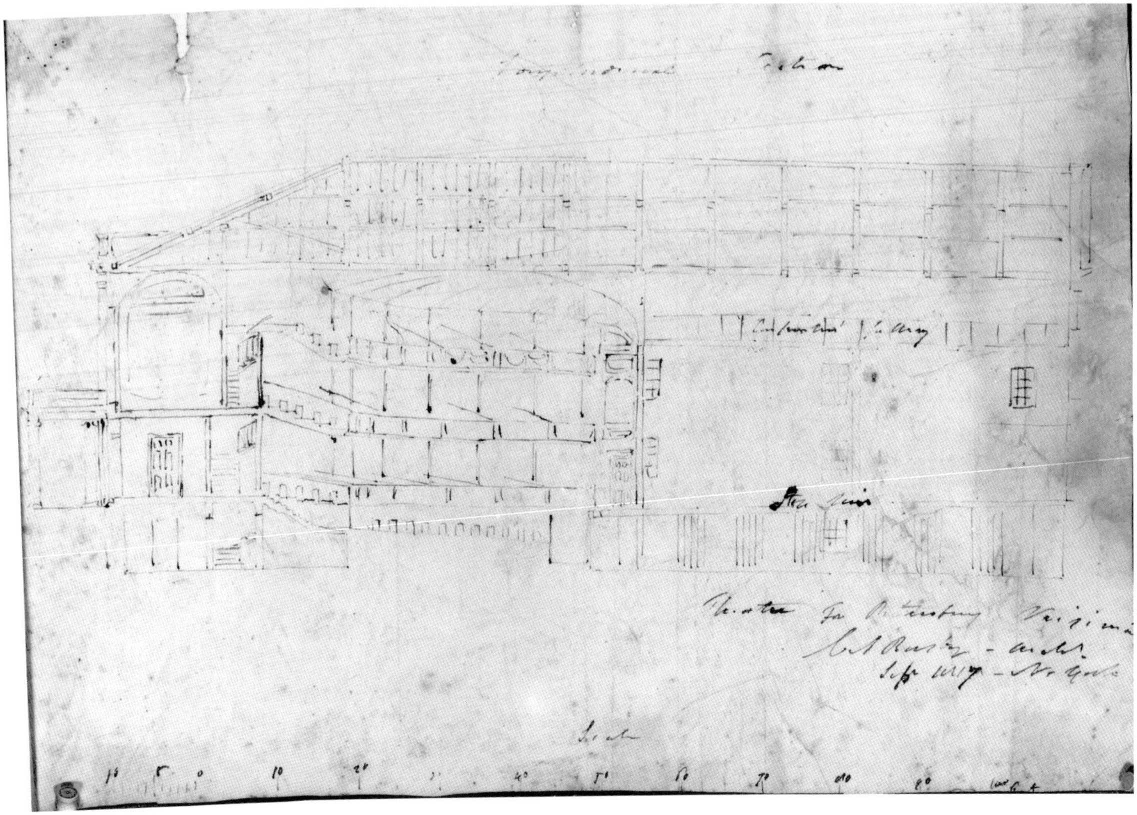

23
Section of the Bollingbrook Theatre, Petersburg, Virginia, 1817.

fondness for investigation, has subsequently impelled me to study the progressive history of mechanical projectors of the steam-engine, to the more finished works of Fulton."(19)

Robert Fulton (1765-1815) had first demonstrated the steamboat on the Hudson River as recently as 1807. Steam-powered navigation was thus still in its infancy with great scope for improvement. Busby was intrigued by the problems of friction and resistance in water which resulted in the slow speed achieved by steamboats. His solution was to improve the waterwheel by using upright paddles, thus giving a motion analogous to amphibians. He produced a wheel model of his invention and, after showing it to the members of the New-York Literary and Philosophical Society, constructed a full-size wheel to his special design.(20) He then tried it out on the York ferry. It failed. He was undeterred, "convinced...that the benignity of the great Creator would not have *denied* to man, an application of power bestowed, almost without exception, on the most minute aquatic animal."(21)

To lessen the water resistance, he hit on the idea of placing his paddle-wheel in a "causeway": an inclined section where the water flow was lessened at one end. In the spring of 1818 he tested his theory by building a mechanically driven boat, 80 feet long and 14 feet wide. Its success is unrecorded, although the vertical paddles must have been seen to have some advantage since two years later, in Britain, Busby's design was stolen and patented by someone else.(22)

Besides inventing a new paddle-wheel, Busby also made inventions in other scientific fields during his stay in America. One device was for what he called a "pocket perspectograph", a small instrument to aid artists in rendering accurate perspectives. Similarly, Busby presented the Literary and Philosophical Society with a machine, invented soon after his arrival, which allowed anyone not versed in perspective to take correct views of even the most complex objects.(23) These optical instruments gained Busby membership of the Society.

The field of perspective appealed to Busby's knowledge and appreciation of the close links between science and art. In much the same way, he delved into the technical details of construction, another field where technology and art meet. In America, Busby embarked upon a study of bridge construction and with his usual eagerness, he measured and recorded three well-known structures. These drawings were engraved on his return to England.

The most ambitious of these measured drawings was made in 1819. It was for the bridge crossing the Delaware River at Trenton, New Jersey.(24) (Fig.24) This wooden struc-

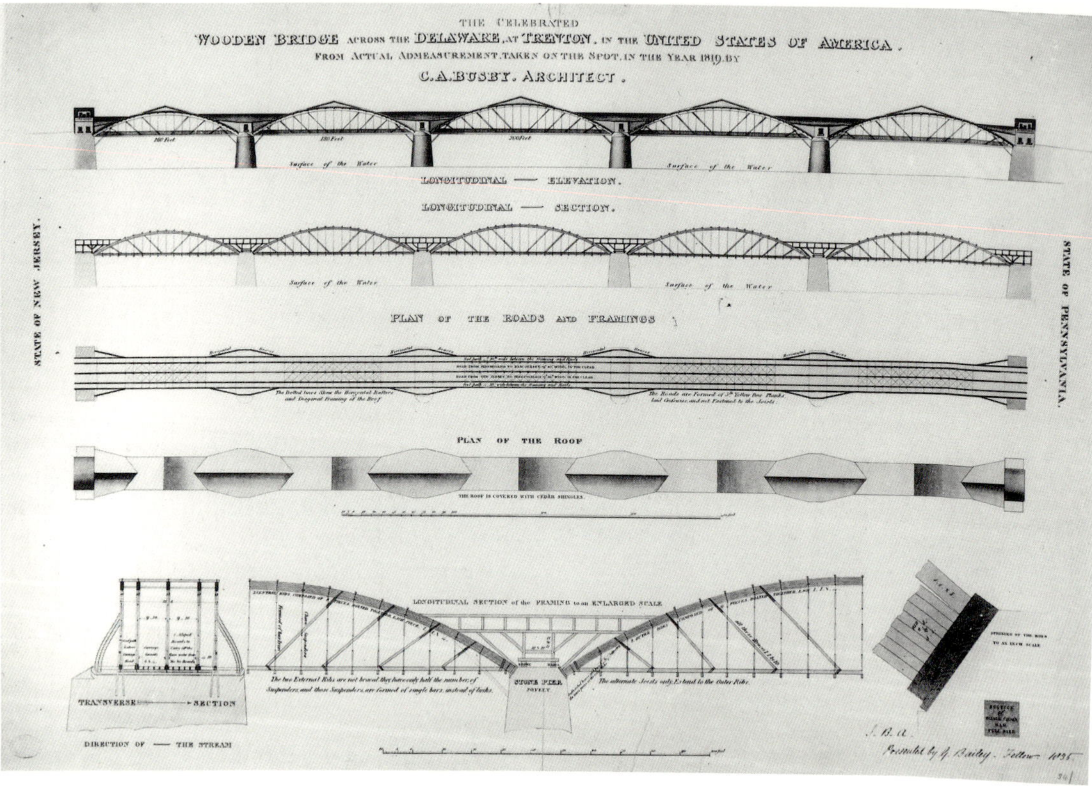

24
Engraving of the Trenton Bridge, New Jersey, as measured by Busby in 1819.

25
Engraving of the Schuylkill Bridge, Philadelphia, as measured by Busby.

ture with a length of more than 1000 feet consisted of five arched spans from which were suspended iron chains and links holding up the carriageway beneath. Busby drew an elevation and sections, and detailed the construction.

In Philadelphia, Busby measured and drew the two covered wooden bridges spanning the Schuylkill River. The oldest of these, the Permanent Bridge - known by this name because it replaced one built on pontoons - had been raised by Timothy Palmer in 1805.(25) (Fig.25) It was triple arched, with a simple trussing system, which although hidden by cladding was exposed for inspection in Busby's print. Entrance at either end of the bridge was through small temple-like toll houses similar to those at each end of the other Philadelphia bridge which Busby measured - the Upper Schuylkill Bridge.(26) (Fig.26)

26
Engraving of the Upper Schuylkill Bridge, Philadelphia, as measured by Busby.

27
Busby's measured drawing of Washington Hall, Philadelphia, designed by Robert Mills in 1814.

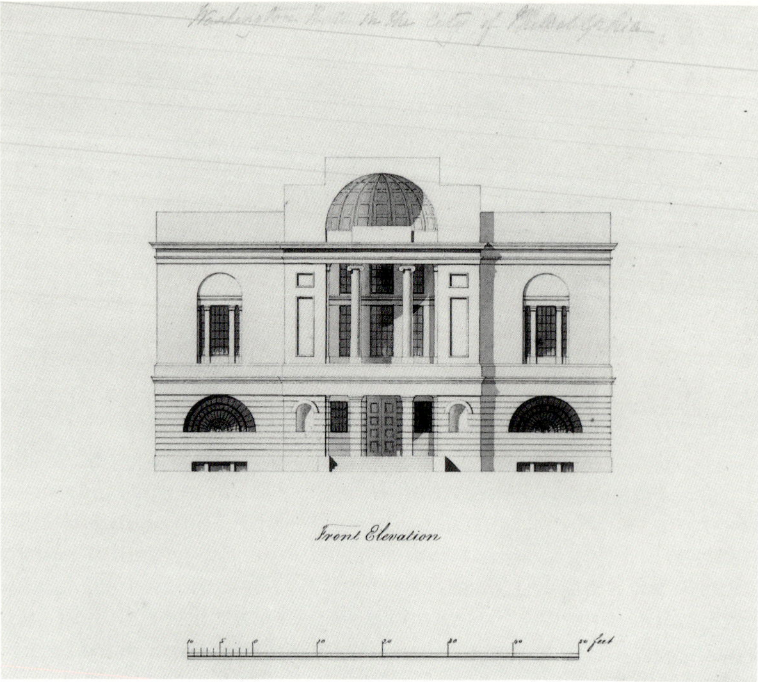

Ledoux's Hôtel Grimard of 1772. As Washington Hall burned down in 1823, Busby's drawing of the building is a measured record of great rarity.

It is very likely that Busby met Mills. The two men had much in common: both were involved in canal building and interested in the progressive role architecture could play in social reform, especially as it affected the designs of penitentiaries.(28)

As Busby criss-crossed the eastern seaboard of America, he visited the principal state prisons and penitentiaries of Massachusetts, Connecticut, New York, New Jersey, Pennsylvania, Maryland and Virginia. As with bridges, he measured and drew these penal establishments with the hope of publishing at a later date.(29) It is unfortunate that the book did not find enough backers as Busby's comprehensive examination of the American system of imprisonment would have broadened the debate on penal reform.

Busby recorded both the horrific conditions and the relatively enlightened approaches to prison design that he witnessed. A plan of one of the worst American prisons is all that survives of Busby's grim tour to the New Gate Prison at Simsbury, near Hartford, Connecticut,(30) (Fig.28) a former copper mine where prisoners were shackled both day and night.(31)

It was undoubtedly Trumbull who proposed Busby's introduction to his close friend,

The toll booths and sheathing of the Upper Bridge, however, were designed by one of America's foremost architects, Robert Mills (1781-1855), who all but encircled the end pavilions with freestanding columns in a classical spirit. Mills had only been responsible for the external design, the technology of America's longest single span of 340 feet had been the work of Lewis Wernog, a German engineer.

The Upper Schuylkill Bridge was one of two structures in Philadelphia by Robert Mills which Busby is known to have measured and drawn. The other was Washington Hall. Busby made a pen and wash drawing of the front elevation.(27) (Fig.27) The hall, designed in 1814 and completed in 1816, was a very elegant example of the American Federal style based strongly on such French prototypes as the architect Charles Bulfinch (1763-1844). Living in Washington since his appointment as architect to the United States Capitol in 1817, Bulfinch was an eminent figure in American architecture. When Busby met him in 1819, Bulfinch was putting the finishing touches to his designs for completing the Capitol Building. Busby, inveterate recorder as he was, produced a plan and elevation of the Capitol in two stages. (Figs. 29 & 30) First he measured and drew the wings of the building which had survived the maleficent arson attack by the British in August 1814. Then, working from a contemporary set of Bulfinch's design drawings, he constructed the missing central section.(32)

But soon after Busby made his drawings of the Capitol, Bulfinch had a change of mind; Busby's record is therefore not as the building was executed. Instead of constructing the design Busby had seen, Bulfinch reverted to a variant of the original 1790s scheme by Dr William Thornton, the building's first architect. Busby's documentation of Bulfinch's intentions - which has survived in the form of aquatints engraved by Busby on his return to

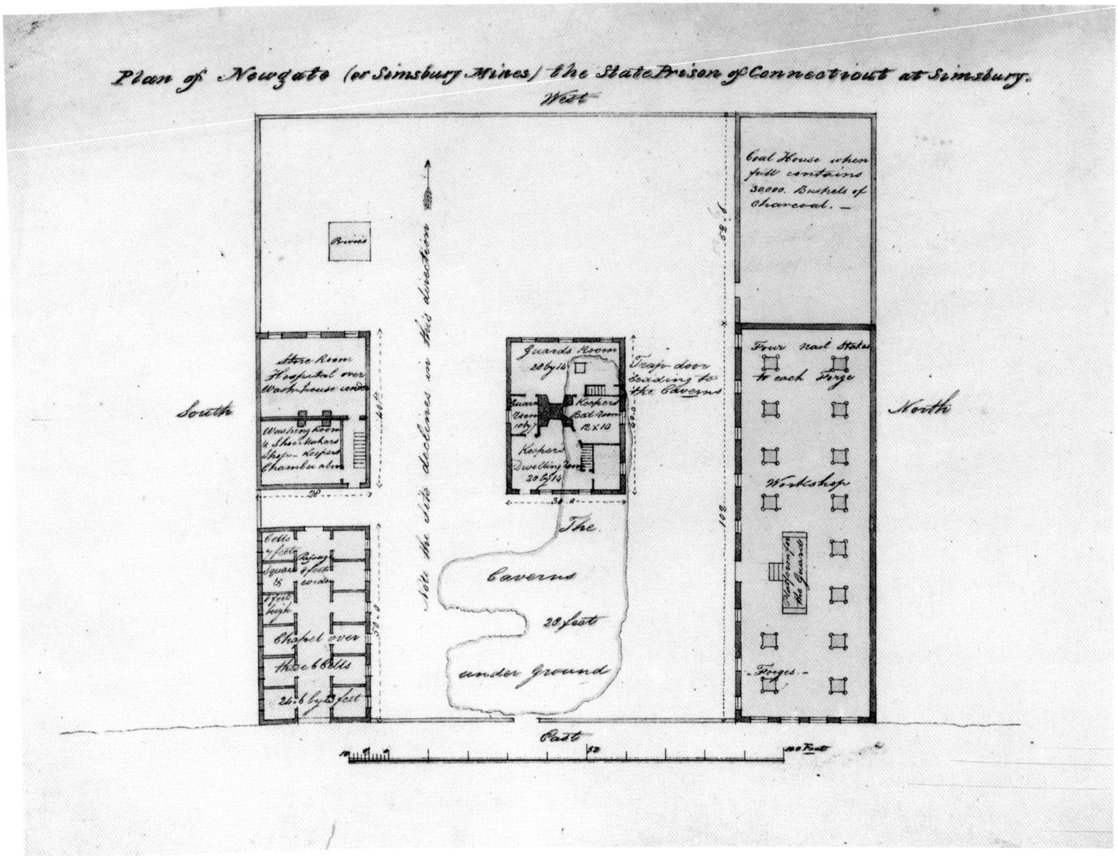

28
Measured plan of the Connecticut State Prison, Simsbury. Busby visited and drew most of the principal prisons in the northern United States.

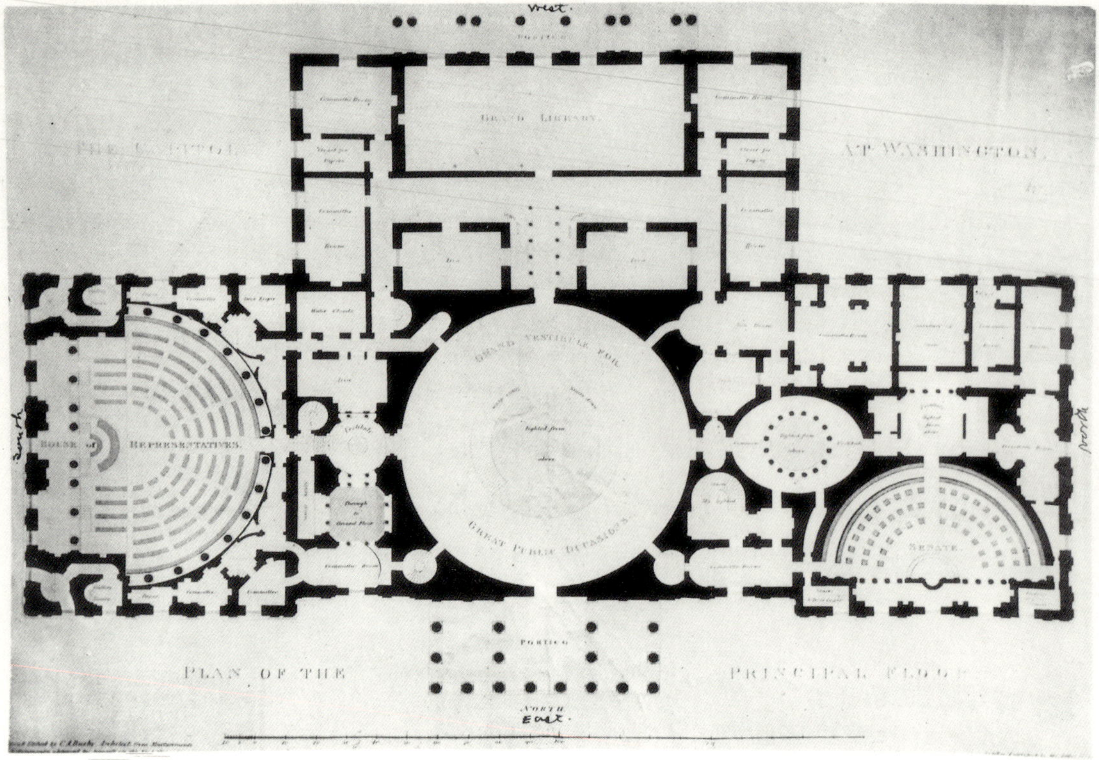

29
An engraving of the plan of the principal storey of the Capitol Building, Washington, made by Busby and based upon Bulfinch's unexecuted scheme.

England - are the only record of this scheme; all of Bulfinch's drawings for the Capitol have been lost.

Busby left Washington with more than just a record of the Capitol Building, he came away carrying a bit of the building itself: a small piece of Potomac marble, a material discovered by Bulfinch's predecessor, Benjamin Henry Latrobe. This object, along with another stone specimen, a chip of American verd-antique found near Baltimore, Busby sent to John Soane, an omnivorous collector of building materials.(33)

Returning to New York, Busby continued to take an active role in the life of the Institution. During the winter of 1818-19, he delivered a course of lectures on architecture and perspective.(34) And, in a meeting of the Literary and Philosophical Society, he put forward the resolution that the Society take casts in iron, or some other strong material, "of the various organic remains of extinct animals" that had been discovered in America. The suggestion was well received, and a committee was formed comprising Busby, the Society's Vice-President Dr Mitchell, and Dr McNeven.(35)

Travelling, making measured drawings, lecturing, building steamboats, serving on committees - all were very stimulating experiences for Busby, but they were not remunerative. In June 1818, Trumbull lent him 50 dollars, without interest, which Busby

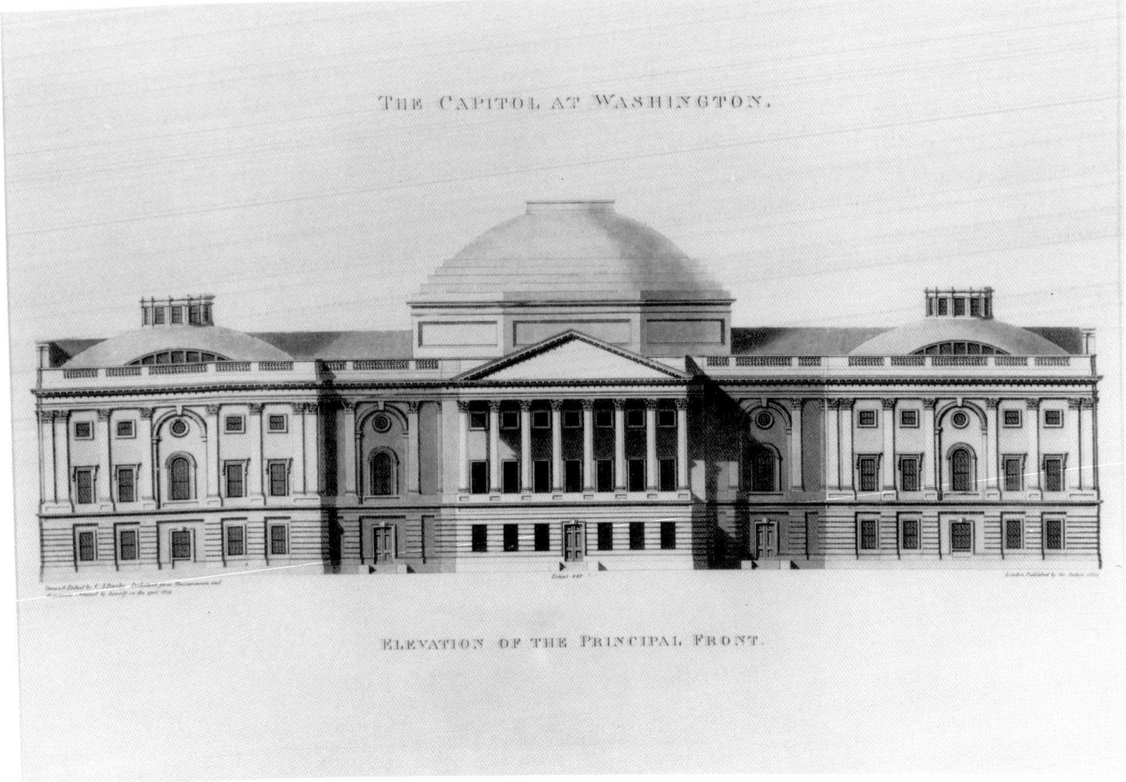

30
The east front of the Capitol Building, Washington, drawn by Busby in 1819 and then engraved by him in 1823.

promised to return in 12 months. But Busby's finances remained strained, and he was unable to repay Trumbull for many more years.(37)

On his travels, Busby visited the inventor Benjamin Dearborn in Brighton, Massachusetts, and examined and sketched parts of Dearborn's weighing machine - a novel contraption for obtaining accurate readings of very heavy as well as light goods. Busby launched a campaign for its universal adoption. Calling himself "an English engineer", Busby wrote to the *New York National Advocate* lauding Dearborn's Proportional Balance.(36)

Busby continued to exhibit at the American Academy, no doubt in the hope of gaining architectural commissions. He never exhibited any of his American work, submitting instead polished drawings he had brought with him. At the second 1817 exhibition, he selected the designs for a conservatory and pheasantry he had erected at Somerley for Henry Baring, his design for Gwrych Castle, and his Southampton Chapel drawing. The following year he revived student drawings that he had shown at the Royal Academy more than a dozen years previously: the view of Westminster Abbey and Worcester Cathedral. And in 1819, Busby exhibited ten of his designs for villas and country houses.(38)

In the middle of 1819 the United States suffered a financial panic and an economic crash. Many farmers and businesses went under. Moreover, New York was hit by a yellow fever epidemic that year. For Busby, this must have seemed the opportune time to return to England. On 9 June 1819 he attended his last meeting at the Institution. And on 10 August he wrote to the painter Alexander Robertson, Secretary of the American Academy of Fine Arts, tendering his single share in the Academy - members being obliged to purchase a share at $25 - to a New York merchant, Joseph Sterlitz.(39)

Charles Augustin Busby had spent more than two years in America. Unlike his fellow English architects who had moved permanently to the United States, men like Benjamin Latrobe and John Haviland, he did not have a profound influence upon the architectural scene. On the contrary, American building and technology influenced *his* work. Busby was one of the first to introduce the British to American architectural and engineering developments.

CHAPTER THREE

RETURN TO ENGLAND 1820 - 1823

After his return from America, Busby set about looking for employment. He had wished to remain independent, but his poor financial situation drove him to work for another architect. In May 1820 his friend, the sculptor J.G. Bubb, introduced him to Francis Goodwin (1784-1835) who was running a busy London architectural office. Goodwin was one of the principal beneficiaries of the 1818 Parliamentary act that delegated to the Church Commissioners the task of distributing one million pounds among highly populated parishes in need of churches. Goodwin was a tough, and at times, unscrupulous businessman, who fought hard to win his church commissions. In Goodwin's office, Busby helped prepare copy drawings, correct originals and make working drawings for chapels in growing communities: he worked on Holy Trinity, Bordesley near Birmingham; St Paul, Portsea near Southsea, Hampshire; and St Peter, Ashton-Under-Lyme, Lancashire.(1)

When Goodwin found himself restricted by the Church Commissioners from taking on more than six churches at a time, he turned to his clerks and fellow architects, offering to give them his plans if they would put them forward in their own names. The fees would be shared, but Goodwin's name was to be kept out of the transaction. Goodwin and Busby came to just such an arrangement over several churches.

Goodwin, however, assigned these promised churches to other architects. This deceit together with his inability to pay Busby's salary at the end of the year's contract induced Busby to leave and set up on his own. He moved to 18 London Street, just off Fitzroy Square, which he furnished with desks, stools and drawing boards lent by Goodwin. Angry as he was with his former employer, Busby remained on speaking terms with him, hoping still for church commissions.

Meanwhile, Busby had been making the rounds, lobbying local committees in the north of England who were considering erecting new churches under the Act of 1818. In spite of Goodwin's interference, Busby won two appointments during the spring of 1821: at Quarry Hill in Leeds, and at Oldham. Goodwin, exasperated at Busby's success, decided to have nothing more to do with him and broke off relations.

Busby began preparing finished drawings for his two churches which in style resembled one another with their tall gothic lines, west tower, and triple porched entrances. And, despite the setback of his earlier structural collapse, he decided to experiment further with iron trusses.

As required, he submitted his designs to the three principal architects of the Office of Works - John Soane, Robert Smirke and John Nash - who acted as official adjudicators in matters relating to the New Churches. Soane was not at the meeting when Smirke and Nash rejected Busby's two churches on the basis that the iron roofs would be weak.

Busby set about an intense campaign of defence of his roofs. He sent a sketch drawing of his proposed design to eight well-known London engineers, asking for their opinions. All replied, confirming the strength and durability of the iron structures. "If any thing," wrote John Millington, Professor of Mechanics at the Royal Institution, "I think them stronger than necessary."(2) But the Church Commissioners still upheld the judgement of Smirke and Nash.

Busby next wrote directly to the two architects, attempting to convince them of their mistaken decision. Although their replies were polite, with Smirke admitting that "my judgment in regard to them may have been wrong", the matter now lay with the Church Commissioners. And the Commissioners would not budge from their decision.

Desperately, Busby attempted to win Soane over by sending him copies of the engineers' testimonials. Presuming that Soane had not supported Smirke and Nash, Busby pleaded with him "to state that you have not lent the powerful authority of your name to their opinion to which my interest and my reputation have been sacrifised."(3) Soane remained out of the fracas.

Busby's next move, in the spring of 1822, was to publish the whole of the correspondence between himself, the supporting engineers, Smirke and Nash in an attempt to reveal the iniquitous situation. (Fig.31)He sent copies of this broadsheet - which included advertisements for his Trenton Bridge print and his intention to publish a volume of American prison designs - to a number of leading architects and every Member of Parliament.(4)

In his final assault, he took on the Archbishop of Canterbury, threatening to expose clerical irregularities between Goodwin's office and the Church Commission. When challenged, however, Busby backed down.

Undaunted, Busby secured the commission to build the parish church of Maidenhead, Berkshire: the Church of St Andrew and St Mary Magdalene. In December 1822, he submitted a set of three alternative designs for approval to the local building committee.(5) Their choice lay between three Gothic variants; the main body of the church, with its polygonal altar end, remained similar in all the designs, with only the west front receiving a graduating degree of elaboration. (Figs.32, 33 & 34)

The material structure of the roof was not shown on the drawings, but it must have been conventional to have passed the three Office of Works architects. The church, as built, was closest in design to the grandest of the schemes. The plan, however, was slightly modified, with the tower, including its clock, set to the side of the polygonal apse. During its life, the church never suffered from structural roof problems; but built on poor subsoil, the walls subsided and weakened, necessitating tie-rods and the eventual rebuilding of the east end in 1877.(6) So dangerous did the structural weakness become, with the a split in the wall running from top to bottom, that the decision to demolish was taken in 1964.

In early 1823, Busby came the closest he would ever get to building a bridge when he was placed third in a competition to find a design for rebuilding London Bridge.(7) Busby's scheme has not survived, but undoubtedly his study of American bridges was an influence. Ironically, the 45 entries in the

WEST ELEVATIONS,

OF THE INTENDED

CHURCHES

AT

LEEDS, AND OLDHAM,

UNANIMOUSLY

APPROVED BY THE

LOCAL COMMITTEES

ACTING UNDER AUTHORITY FROM

HIS MAJESTY'S COMMISSIONERS

For Building Additional Churches.

A. D. 1821.

C. A. BUSBY, ARCHITECT,

OFFICE, No. 13,

LONDON STREET, FITZROY SQUARE.

C. A. Busby, delt. OLDHAM. 70 Feet Front.

Engraved on Wood, by H. White, 15, St. John's Lane.

LEEDS. 70 Feet Front. *C. A. Busby, delt.*

A STATEMENT OF THE PROCEEDINGS BEFORE HIS MAJESTY'S COMMISSIONERS FOR BUILDING ADDITIONAL CHURCHES, AND OTHER PERSONS, IN RELATION TO THE INTENDED CHURCHES AT LEEDS, AND OLDHAM, 1821, 1822.

To render the following particulars distinctly intelligible, it will be proper to commence by observing that, on the 30th of May, 1818, an Act of Parliament was passed, entitled, "*An Act for the Building and the promoting the Building of additional Churches in populous Parishes;*" and that a million sterling was granted, in aid of that important object.

By this Act, His Majesty was empowered, to appoint an unlimited number of Commissioners, "*any five of whom might act in execution of the powers of this Act.*"—The present Commissioners are, the Archbishops of Canterbury, and York; the Bishops of London, Chester, Litchfield and Coventry, Winchester, and Killaloe; the Earls Eldon, Harrowby, Liverpool, and Hardwick; Viscount Sidmouth; Lords Grenville, Kenyon, Colchester, and Stowell; the Right Honorables Sir John Nicoll, C. Manners Sutton, N. Vansittart, C. Bathurst, and W. Huskisson; the Dean of Westminster; the Archdeacons Wollaston, Cambridge, Pott, and Eyre; the Reverend J. Headlam; F. Burton, and Joshua Watson, Esqrs; and Colonel Stephenson. The Commissioners have authority to appoint a Secretary (George Jenner, Esq.), and Clerk (Mr. Wm. Richardson), to order Surveys, Reports, &c. and are required to draw up rules for their proceedings; with "*power to alter or vary any such regulations, and to make any further additional regulations, as they may deem expedient;*" subject to the approval of His Majesty in Council. Other clauses render it imperative upon Parishes, unprovided with accommodation for the spiritual instruction of a certain proportion of their population, (and possessed of sufficient means,) to provide seites for new Churches; but, giving the Commissioners full power to provide both seites, and Churches, where the pecuniary circumstances of the Inhabitants, may seem to render such a course advisable.

To carry this Act into operation, the Commissioners have found it convenient to refer the details of proceedings to a Committee, consisting of five Members; but of whom frequently not more than three, and sometimes only two, have leisure to attend. The Members of this Committee are, the Right Honourable Lord Kenyon, the Reverend Archdeacons Wollaston, and Cambridge, Joshua Watson, Esq. and Colonel Stephenson, the Surveyor-General of His Majesty's Office of Works. The resolutions of the Committee are necessarily submitted to the Board of Commissioners, in order to their legalization, But as the Committee consists of Gentlemen, who are themselves leading Commissioners, the result of their representations to the Board may generally be anticipated. Such, indeed, is the occasional difficulty of procuring a sufficient attendance of Members, on *board-days*, that the Messenger is sometimes dispatched, after the appointed hour of meeting has elapsed, to urge the presence of one, or two, in order to collect the quorum of five, required by the Act. It must, however, in candour be stated, that the Board-room is, in some instances, honoured with a more numerous assemblage, and that a fuller attendance at Committees is not uncommon.

During the course of proceedings under the Act, it has generally been found that Parishes, whose claims have obtained a preference, were able, and willing to provide seites; and in such cases it has been usual for a number of the most respectable Inhabitants to associate themselves under the sanction of the Incumbent, or officiating Minister, in order to form what is termed a *Local Committee*, to negociate with His Majesty's Commissioners. It has also been customary with the Board of Commissioners, after having approved of the seites, respectively, to direct these Local Committees to furnish them with plans for the intended Church, or Churches, as the case may be. In some instances the Local Committees have, consequently, invited a professional competition among Architects, in order to make a selection; in others, they have proceeded to nominate an architect, and to instruct him to prepare designs. The first course was pursued at Leeds, in Yorkshire; the latter at Oldham, in Lancashire; and, in both these cases, I had the satisfaction to find my plans adopted, under very flattering circumstances of professional approbation.

Both my designs were duly forwarded by the Local Committees of Leeds, and Oldham, to the Board in London; and came regularly under consideration, in the Spring of 1821. The peculiarities of each Church were elucidated in strict conformity to the following particulars; which are reprinted from one of the cards, circulated by the Secretary of the Board, among the Local Committees.

"PARTICULARS

"*Required, when Plans and Elevations of a Church or*
"*Chapel are submitted to the Board.*
"Ground Plan of the Building.
"*The Altar being placed at the East end.*
"Plan of Galleries, *if any.*
"Elevations.
"The form of the Roof, as intended to be framed,
"*figured.*
"Longitudinal and Transverse Sections.
"*All in plain Indian Ink.*
"*Scale, one-eighth of an Inch to a Foot.*
"Number of Persons to be seated in Pews.
"Ditto, in Free Seats.
"*Pews to be not less than Two Feet Ten Inches*
"*wide, and Twenty Inches to be allowed to*
"*each Person.*
"*Free Seats to be Two Feet Three Inches wide,*
"*and Twenty Inches to be allowed for Adults.*
"A Specification, and a detailed Estimate of the
"Work, and Prices of the different Articles of
"Building."

My designs were received by the Commissioners, in a manner extremely gratifying to my feelings. The Bishop of Chester, in particular, was pleased to observe to me, that he prefered the one intended for Oldham, in his Lordship's diocese, to any he had yet seen, among those already before the Board. The plans, specifications, and estimates, were subsequently refered to Mr. Edward Mawley, Surveyor to the Commissioners, for verification; that Gentleman examined them in due rotation with the plans of other Churches, and eventually made a favourable report upon them; informing me, at the same time, in answer to my particular enquiries, that, when working drawings were required, I should receive instructions from the Board. The whole were now refered by the Committee to the Surveyor-General, (one of their own Members) in order to procure a Report upon the proposed construction, from MR. SOANE, MR. NASH, and MR. SMIRKE, the three Architects attached to his office.

Being in attendance at the Board-room, (No. 12, Great George Street, Westminster) when the Reports, from the Architects of the Office of Works, came under the consideration of the Church Commissioners, on the 11th of September, 1821, (for a very considerable period had been occupied in all the previous proceedings) I was called before the three Gentlemen, Mr. Archdeacon Wollaston, the Surveyor-General, and Mr. Watson, then sitting in Committee. Mr. Archdeacon Wollaston, as Chairman, addressed me; saying, he was sorry to communicate, that a Report of a most serious nature, had been made by the Architects of the Surveyor-General's Office; and the more so, as it would unavoidably impair the confidence which would otherwise have been placed, by His Majesty's Commissioners, in my professional capability. That it behoved the Committee to proceed with caution, and that it had, therefore, been already resolved to send copies of the following Report, to the Local Committees of Leeds, and Oldham, in order that they might be apprized of what was going forward,

REPORT.—OLDHAM.

"The Drawings given for this Church do not "describe the intended construction sufficiently, to "enable us to report upon the whole of it; but the "Roof, according to the drawing of one of the "Principals, would be extremely weak and insecure.

REPORT.—LEEDS.

"The remarks made upon the drawings for the "preceding Church, apply in every respect to these.
(Signed) "JOHN NASH.
"ROBERT SMIRKE."
(But not Signed by Mr. Soane. C. A. B.)

In reply to this serious, and unexpected address, it is sufficiently obvious that I could, at the moment, do nothing more than aver my surprise, express my undiminished confidence in the proposed construction, and offer to prove its stability on the spot, if the plans (then in the room) were laid upon the table. This was objected to, and I was informed by Mr. Archdeacon Wollaston, that, if I could offer any thing in support, or explanation, at the next meeting, it would probably be attended to.

Satisfied that the Roofs (constructed in a great measure of iron) did not merit the censure thus hastily passed upon them, I took immediate steps to obtain the opinions of some of the first Architects, and practical Engineers, on the subject; but without informing them from whence objections had proceeded. I was consequently favoured with the following corroborative communications, from eight professional gentlemen (the whole number consulted) in the short period of five days.

"Sir, "Lambeth, Sept. 13, 1821.
"Having examined the sketches of two roofs, "and heard your explanations of them, I have no "doubt but they are more than sufficiently strong, "and likely to stand as long as the materials last: "having fixed several upon a similar principle, "which have been standing several years in the "most perfect manner.
"With respect, I remain, your's, &c.
(Signed) "HENRY MAUDSLAY."
"C. A. Busby, Esq."

"My Dear Sir, "Grange Road, Bermondsey, Sept. 14, 1821.
"I have examined the sketch of the principal for "a roof, which you left me yesterday, and instead "of taking your estimated weight, viz. eighteen "tons, six hundred weight, as that which each prin- "cipal will have to bear, I have supposed it to be "twenty tons—

	F.	I.
"The span, as per drawing,	29	0
"The perpendicular rise,	12	4

"The length of the king-post, 5 0 in. in.
"The lower principal of cast iron, $12 \times 1\frac{1}{2}$,
"equal 18 area the wrought Iron Bar,
"$5 \times \frac{3}{4}$ and allowing for key-holes, I have
"taken its sectional area at 3 inches.
"And I find, on a rough estimate, that a princi- "pal so constructed, of sound materials, would bear "above a 100 tons, provided the king-post be strong "enough. Upon the latter I could make no calcu- "lation, as I had not the dimensions.
"I am, dear Sir, your's very truly,
"Mr. Busby. (Signed) "BRYAN DONKIN."

"Sir, "Pimlico, 14th Sept. 1821. 9 P.M.
"I have not found time to enter into the calcula- "tion (I promised you this morning) of what the "cast iron principals, of your proposed Roofs of the "two Churches, you are about to build in Yorkshire, "will actually bear with safety; but judging from "various examples I have seen, and in particular "some Roofs, erected by my friend Mr. Maudslay, "in his own works, (which are upon a somewhat "similar principle) I have no hesitation to pro- "nounce them fully adequate to any weight they "can be subjected to, by the purlins and covering: "indeed, according to my view of the case, you "have been rather profuse in the employment of "material, provided not more that Eighteen Tons, 6 "cwt. (as you state) be the load which each principal "has to sustain. I send you these brief remarks, "understanding that a speedy reply is essential to "you. I am, Sir, your's faithfully,
"Mr. C. A. Busby. (Signed) "TIMY. BRAMAH."

"Dear Sir, "6, Leigh Street, Burton Crescent. 14th, September, 1821.
"I have examined the drawings of the two Roofs "you sent me, for the Churches at Leeds and Old- "ham; and having, as you know, been very much "accustomed to the use of cast iron, I have no "hesitation in saying, that I conceive them amply "sufficient for the purpose for which they are in- "tended; and, that you need not be under any fear "of their giving way; if any thing, I think them "stronger than necessary.
"I am, dear Sir, your's very truly,
"JOHN MILLINGTON.
Civil Engineer, and Professor of Mechanics in the Royal Institution.
"C. A. Busby, Esq."

"Sir, "69, High Holborn, 14 Sept. 1821.
"The plan and capacity of the Iron Roofs, which "you have exhibited to me, appear to have no material "defect, but the circumstance of their being, in my "estimation, much too heavy and strong. I am "making now, three large roofs, considerably lighter, "and much greater span, and I have no fear what- "ever of their durability or strength.
"I am, Sir, your's respectfully,
"Mr. C. A. Busby. (Signed) "A. GALLOWAY."

"Dear Sir, "39, Finsbury Square, 15th Sept. 1821.
"I am sorry that my engagements to-day pre- "vented me from looking at the sketch of the prin- "cipal of your Roof, until the last moment you gave "me. From the superficial view I have, however, "taken of it, I have no doubt of its being sufficiently "strong, for any covering of moderate weight, and "calculating upon the distance of the principals, "not exceeding 16 feet 8 inches.
"I remain, your's very truly,
(Signed) "J. WALKER."
(Architect and Engineer to Vauxhall Bridge.)
"C. A. Busby, Esq." (C. A. B.)

"Dear Sir, "Chelsea, September 15, 1821.
"I have inspected the drawing of your cast iron "roof, which you propose to place over a building "with a span of 29 feet. I have no hesitation in "stating, that it is more than adequate to the strength "required for supporting the roof of that building.
"I am, dear Sir, your's very truly,
(Signed) "Mc. J. BRUNEL."
(Inventor of the celebrated Block Machine in the Royal Dock-Yard, Portsmouth. C. A. B.)
"Mr. Busby, Architect."

"Sir, "2, Grove Terrace, 17th Sept. 1821.
"I have examined a sketch of a Roof for a Church "which you left for my opinion upon this morning; "and having estimated its strength, it appears to me "that it will be perfectly secure, if executed in a "workman-like manner, of proper materials, and "the iron and wooden parts connected, and braced, "in the way you propose.
"I am, Sir, your most obedient Servant,
(Signed) "THOMAS TREDGOLD."
(Author of the best English Treatise on Carpentry, and Roofs. C. A. B.)
"To Mr. Busby."

At the next meeting of the Church Commissioners, on the 18th of September, 1821, the Secretary was informed, that I was in attendance with some important and satisfactory information, relating to the late Report from Messrs. Nash and Smirke. I was accordingly invited before Mr. Archdeacon Wollaston, and the Surveyor-General, the only gentlemen present, and then setting in Committee.

I prefaced an oral address, by requesting the Report of Messrs. Nash and Smirke might be read, which was accordingly done by the Secretary. Then producing one of the printed cards of particulars, circulated by the authority of the Board, I proved that both sets of plans, specifications, and estimates, had been delivered in strict compliance thereto. I also observed, that since Mr. Mawley, the Surveyor, had been able to render a satisfactory account of the intended Building, from such documents as those already furnished, Messrs. Nash and Smirke might reasonably be expected to find little difficulty in following his example. But that, if I had been informed, or had even understood, that further drawings were required in the present stage of proceedings, I should most undoubtedly have furnished them. That in fact, Mr. Mawley himself, in answer to my enquiries on that subject, had repeatedly told me that further drawings were not wanted, and *would not even be accepted*, till I should receive particular instructions from the Board to produce them.

I then proceeded to animadvert upon that part of the Report which bore upon the Roof. I repeated my former affirmation, that I had not proposed the peculiar construction without due consideration, and was still satisfied, as I had ever been, of its ample solidity. But, that, in consequence of the unexpected objections of Messrs. Nash and Smirke, I had thought it advisable to take the opinions of eight leading Professional Gentlemen, and would proceed to read to the Committee their letters, addressed to me, on the subject. Mr. Archdeacon Wollaston instantly checked me: the Reverend Gentleman observed, that Messrs. Nash and Smirke had volunteered their services, and acted gratuitously, and that it was, therefore, the decided intention of the Church Commissioners, to shield them from professional disputation. That if I had produced an argument, it might have been received; but that the testimonials in my hands were altogether in admissible; he would not even hear the names of their respective authors!

To this I replied, that had the Report itself been of an argumentative nature, I would most readily have disproved it by argument; but that, as it consisted, on the contrary, of an *unqualified assertion*, it could not be better met than in the way I proposed. I trusted, however, as the Reverend Archdeacon was against receiving the papers, it would be conceded to me, that they were of a powerful nature. I also thought it necessary to inform the Committee (lest in consequence of any future inaccurate recollection of dates, I might hereafter appear to have acted in opposition to the Rev. Archdeacon's expressed wish) that I had already sent copies of all the testimonials, to the Local Committees at Leeds, and Oldham. Mr. Archdeacon Wollaston instantly expressed his serious disapproval of the measure. I replied, that it had been rendered *necessary* by the act of the Committee themselves, at their last meeting, when they had directed copies of the Report of Messrs. Nash and Smirke, upon my Plans, to be sent to those places, *where it was calculated to do me great injury*, unless refuted. Mr. Archdeacon Wollaston earnestly inquired whether the Report had actually been sent: the Secretary did not know, but would enquire; and, leaving the room to consult the Clerk, said, on his return, "*it was really gone, according to the order of the last Committee.*"

This explanation seemed conclusive; a desultory discussion ensued, during the course of which some elevated eulogiums were bestowed upon Messrs.

31
The broadsheet published by Busby in 1822 showing his unexecuted designs for churches at Oldham and Leeds.

competition were judged by the Office of Works architects - Nash, Smirke and Soane - but as the competitors submitted their models and drawings anonymously, Busby's identity would not have been revealed until after the judging had taken place.

During this period, Busby managed to find time to continue with his hydraulic experiments. In attempting to determine the resistance of solid bodies in their passage through fluids, Busby hit upon a brilliant method of moving mechanical parts through water in a smooth action. He put his discovery to effect in a most ingenious way - by constructing an hydraulic-powered orrery. (Fig.35)

32
First design for the Church of St Andrew & St Mary Magdalene, Maidenhead, Berkshire, 1822.

33
Second design.

34
Third design.

35
An engraving of a section and plan of Busby's hydraulic orrery. Busby's machine for showing the movement of the planets won the Vulcan Medal at the Royal Society of Arts in 1822.

Busby had no doubt studied the famous Rittenhouse Orrery at the College and Academy of Philadelphia, which had been completed in 1771 by the American clockmaker and pioneer astronomer David Rittenhouse.(8) Busby's orrery was less grand since it did not show the movements of the entire solar system, but rather restricted itself to the sun and the orbits of the earth and moon. Standing above a circular basin of water more than five feet wide, the celestial bodies glided slowly around one another, powered by the passing of water through syphons. The action, as opposed to the jerkiness of the usual clockwork mechanism, was smooth and flowing.(9) When a distinguished group of scientists gathered to watch the orrery in action, one member, the celebrated astronomical-instrument maker Edward Troughton, was moved to exclaim, "I never before saw a uniform motion; it is beautiful."(10)

Busby won the Gold Vulcan Medal in Mechanics from the Royal Society of Arts in 1822 for his hydraulic orrery. As a condition of winning, he made a smaller model than the one he kept in his London Street office, and presented it to the Society.(11)

But the construction of the orrery and the loss of the commissions for the churches at Leeds and Oldham left Busby without much money. He must have been relieved when offered the chance of escaping from London and taking part in a lucrative building scheme.

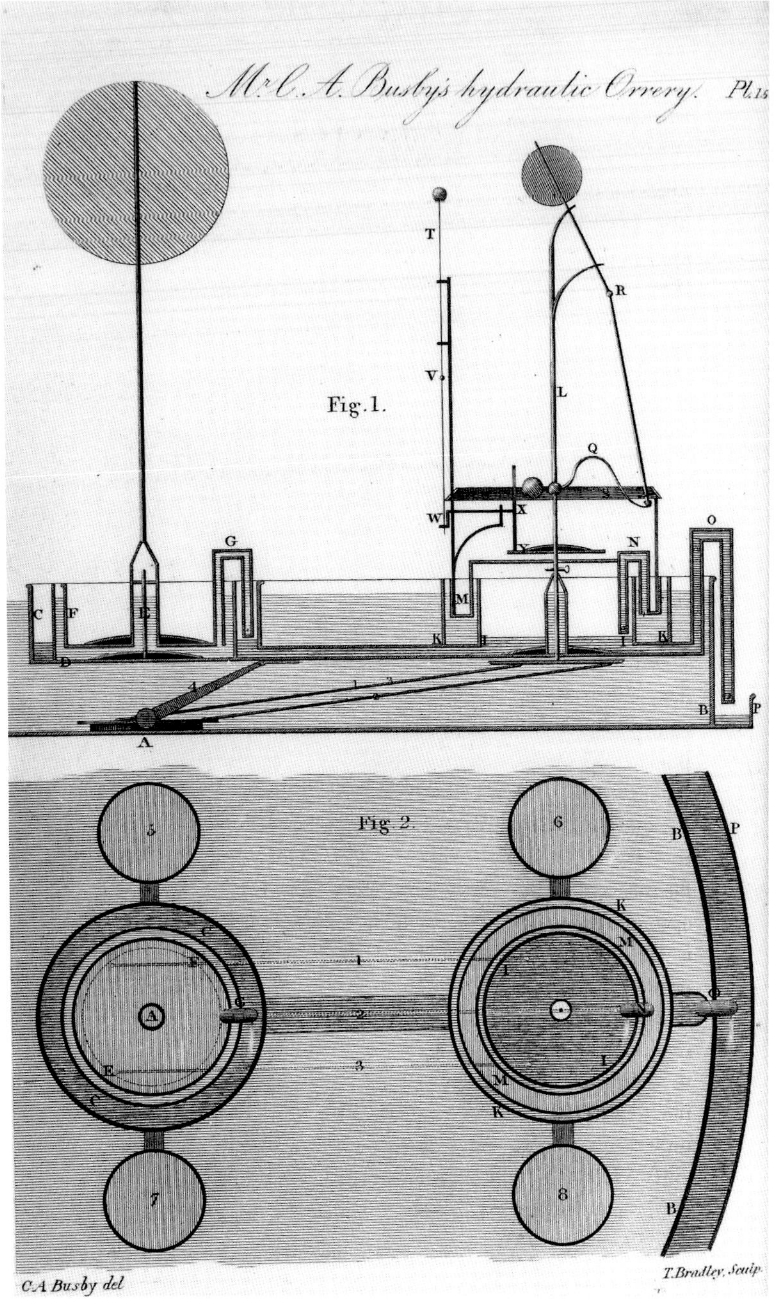

CHAPTER FOUR

BRIGHTON AND HOVE 1823 - 1834

Busby's introduction to a brighter future was probably made through his former client Henry Baring of Somerley, whose sister, Frances, was married to Thomas Read Kemp (1782-1844), a rich Sussex landowner. Kemp, a political radical, had been a Member of Parliament from 1812 until 1816 when he was obliged to give up his seat because, under the influence of his sister-in-law, Harriet Wall (née Baring), he had formed an evangelical sect.(1) In 1823, however, Kemp returned to the established church, and to Parliament. In that year too he persuaded Busby to move to Brighton.

Having decided to build a large housing development on part of his Brighton holdings, Kemp had gone in search of an architect. In the past, he had turned to a local builder, Amon Wilds (1762-1833), and his architect son, Amon Henry (1784-1857), for most of his projects. It had been the Wilds, for example, who had designed Trinity Chapel for Kemp's dissenting congregation. Still wishing to retain the Wilds, but realizing that his new estate might be too large a project for them, he must have thought it prudent to call in an architect with wider experience. No doubt it was at Kemp's suggestion that Busby joined the younger Wilds to form an architectural partnership.

Although the Wilds had moved to Brighton only as recently as 1815, it was in Lewes - the county town of Sussex eight miles from Brighton - that they had first employed their punning architectural trademark: the ammonite capital with volutes of ammonite shells, a decorative variation on the Ionic order first used by George Dance junior. The ammonite, and the motif of a scallop shell, appear constantly in the work of the Wilds, especially the talented Amon Henry.

Charles Augustin Busby and Amon Henry Wilds commenced their architectural partnership in May 1823, although they did not officially record their business until 2 February 1824.(2) With his wife and family, Busby moved to Brighton and into 13 Waterloo Place, a small house in a terrace that formed part of a speculative development the Wilds had been building over the previous few years.(3) A short walk away from his new home was his partner's finest work to date, Hanover Crescent, a series of elegant houses, many with ammonite capitals. In the North Lodge, one of the two small temples guarding the Crescent's entrances, Wilds and Busby set up their office.

The rise of speculative building in Brighton, which had begun a few years prior to Busby's arrival, had been spurred on by the royal, the rich and the famous who had made the town Britain's most fashionable seaside resort. As early as the 1750s, when still a fishing village, Brighton had began to supercede its old rival Bath as Britain's premier spa town. Several advantages weighed in Brighton's favour. As opposed to the day or more journey from London to Bath, the 65 mile carriage ride to Brighton took five to six hours. Gentlemen could readily nip up to town on urgent business and be back with their family and friends the next day. Stories of Brighton's restorative powers for health grew steadily: a quick plunge in the icy waters of the English Channel or an outing in the bracing sea air was said to cure, or at least alleviate, a variety of illnesses, from gout to dropsy.

Brighton's fame had been secured in 1783 when the leader of the fashionable world, George, Prince of Wales (later King George IV), chose to stay regularly during the season - which lasted from October to March - and to build a house in the centre of the town. As George's princely duties grew - taking on the responsibilities of the crown as Regent in 1811 - so too did his small marine villa. Under the direction of the architect Henry Holland and

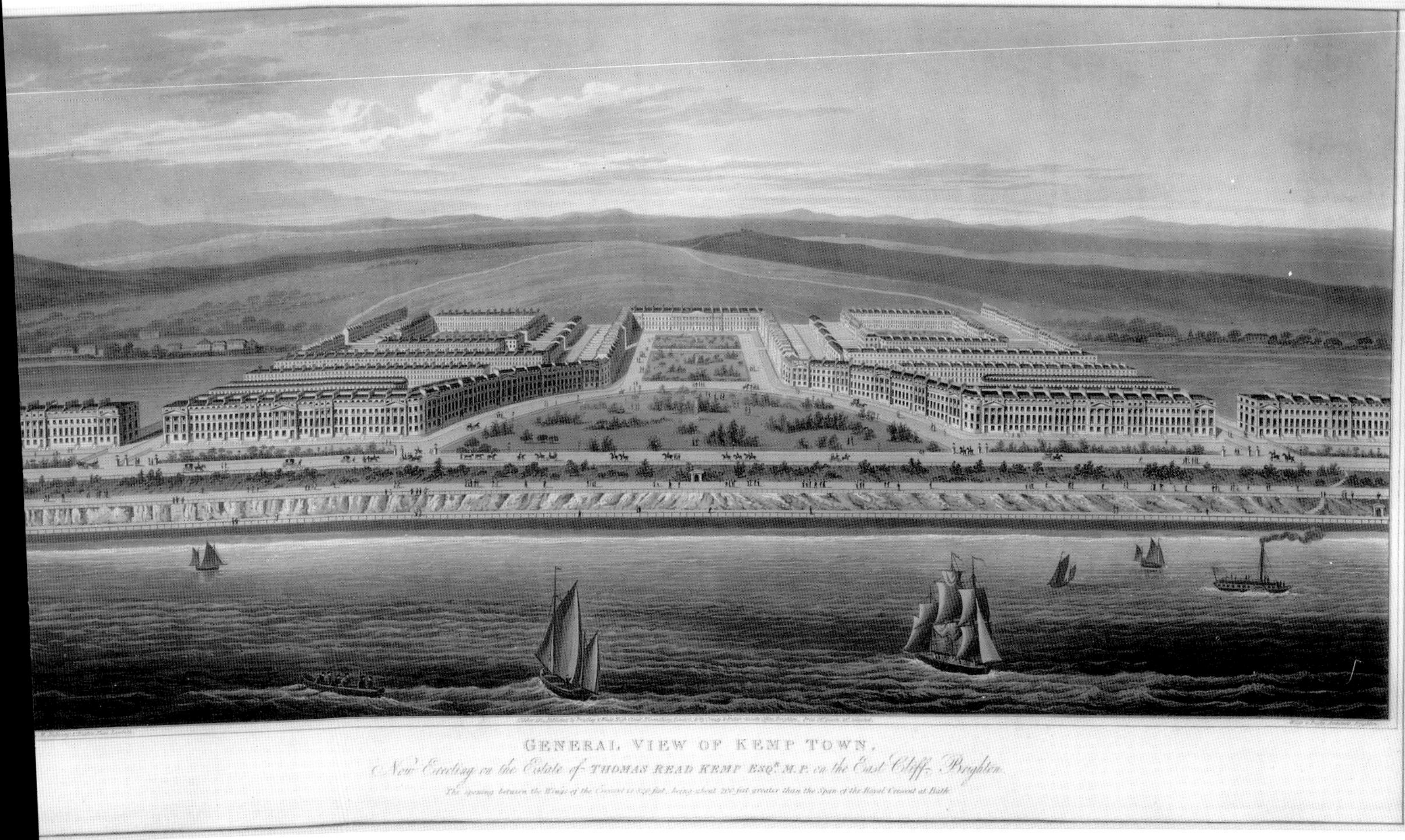

36
Kemp Town, engraved by M. Dubourg in 1824, the year following the start of construction.

then spectacularly under Nash, the Royal Pavilion blossomed into one of the richest and most exotic creations ever conceived.

When Busby arrived in 1823, Brighton's leading resident had been King for three years. The town, with a permanent population of about 25,000 - around the same size as the New York that Busby had left behind - was dominated by the brilliance of the Court and the society that surrounded it. Besides the constant round of balls, dinners and concerts, visitors gathered at the lending libraries, drank the waters at the Chalybeate Spring and the Royal German Spa, played cards and took tea at the assembly rooms, discreetly dipped in the sea, bet at the races, ambled in John Ireland's Royal Pleasure Gardens, rode up onto the gentle slopes of the surrounding South Downs, soaked in the curative waters of a local bathhouse or were treated to a shampoo, as massages were then called. It was a social necessity to be seen promenading or being driven in one's carriage along the seafront and around the green lawns of the Steine opposite the Royal Pavilion.

37
Lewes Crescent, Kemp Town, Brighton.

The ever increasing number of visitors and the growing population of new residents, required more and better accommodation.

Kemp Town was created in the hope of meeting this demand. Early prints of Kemp Town show the ambitious nature of the development as first envisioned. (Fig.36) At the heart of the enterprise, sloping up from the sea, are the curved arms of Lewes Crescent, broken at the top by Sussex Square. Ranging on either side of the crescent, parallel with the coast, are the straight lines of Arundel Terrace to the east and Chichester Terrace to the west. In the original scheme, a series of large inland squares were planned; but these never materialized. Of the 250 houses proposed for the development, 105 were built.

The precedents for the Kemp Town plan lay in the Royal Crescent at Bath and Nash's new stuccoed terraces then going up around Regent's Park in London. But the arrangement in Brighton was unique in its marriage of crescent with square and the transfer of an 18th century town planning concept to the seaside.

When designing Lewes Crescent and Sussex Square, Wilds and Busby had to compensate for the gentle slope of the land as it rose away from the sea. All of Brighton and Hove is built on the slope of the Downs, mainly to an architectural advantage, as it

38
Church of St George, Brighton. Designed by Busby in 1824 to serve as the chapel for Kemp Town.

allows many of the buildings to be seen from the coast and, conversely, for the occupants to glimpse the sea. The sense of theatre and backdrop so important to Regency promenaders and spectators was thus heightened. (Fig.37)

Typical of such large scale developments during the period, the rôle of the architects was to plan the estate and design the façades. The interior arrangements, decoration and supervision of construction were left to the landowner, the builders and the individual purchasers. In the case of Kemp Town, Thomas Cubitt, the finest builder of the late Georgian and early Victorian periods worked closely with T.R. Kemp on the construction, and even took a house in Lewes Crescent.(4)

To serve the new residents of his town, Kemp obtained a private Act of Parliament for erecting a local chapel of ease. This was granted on 3 June 1824.(5) Construction began almost immediately on the Chapel of St George. Busby was the architect, working without his partner. In keeping with the classicism of Kemp Town - although St George's is located more than a quarter of a mile away - Busby returned to his favoured Greek Revival with the external architectural emphasis placed upon the sets of recessed Ionic columns on both the west and east elevations and the tall boxed steeple over the entrance.(6) (Fig.38)

The Chapel of St George was consecrated by the Bishop of Chichester on 30 December 1825, and opened for worship on New Year's Day 1826. During the 1830s it became very popular with the fashionable world, especially Queen Adelaide who worshipped there often.

Contrary to expectation, Kemp Town was not an immediate success. Its location, although attractive, was more than a mile to the east of the town centre. Then, too, just as the new estate was getting under way, the King's visits to Brighton became sporadic, decreasing although by no means stopping the flow of visitors needing housing. Kemp Town also began to feel the effect of the economic fluctuations affecting Britain at this time.

Although by 1828 Lewes Crescent and Sussex Square had acquired a finished appearance, many of the houses were mere façades. In that year, a visitor wrote: "I entered the town, which now, at the period of its birth,

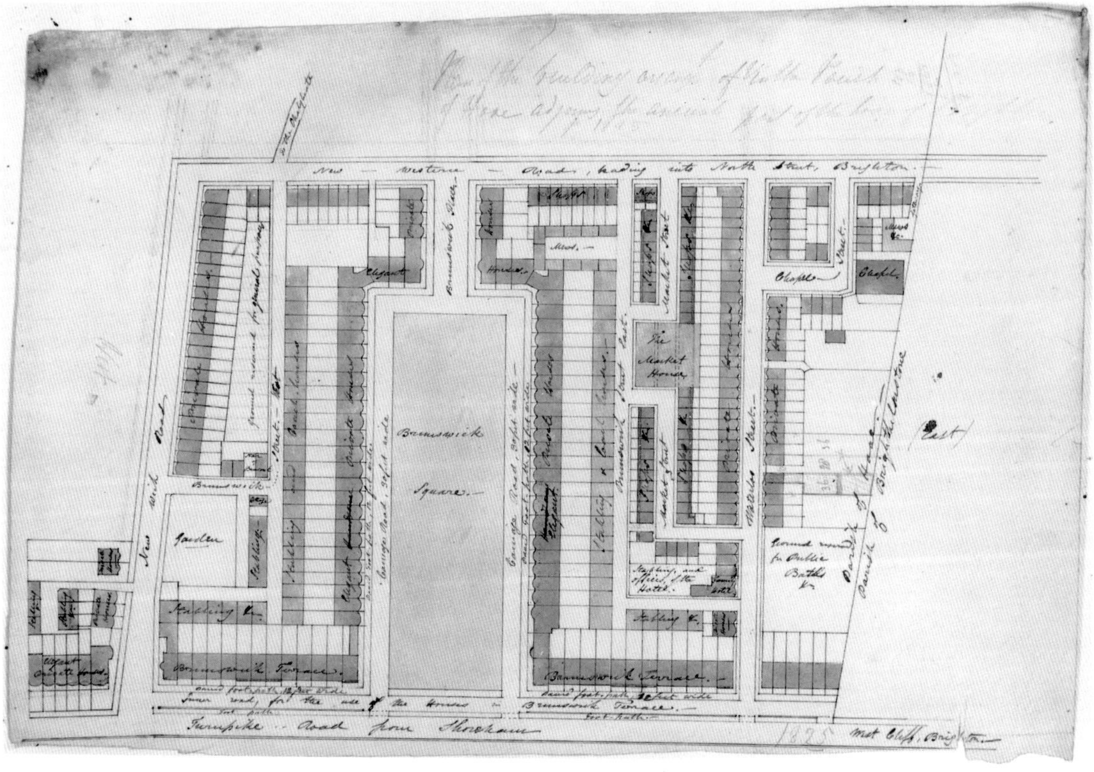

39
An early plan for Brunswick Town, Hove, 1825. Busby's original scheme for terraced housing served by shops, a hotel, chapel and market was an attempt to make the new estate almost independent of Brighton.

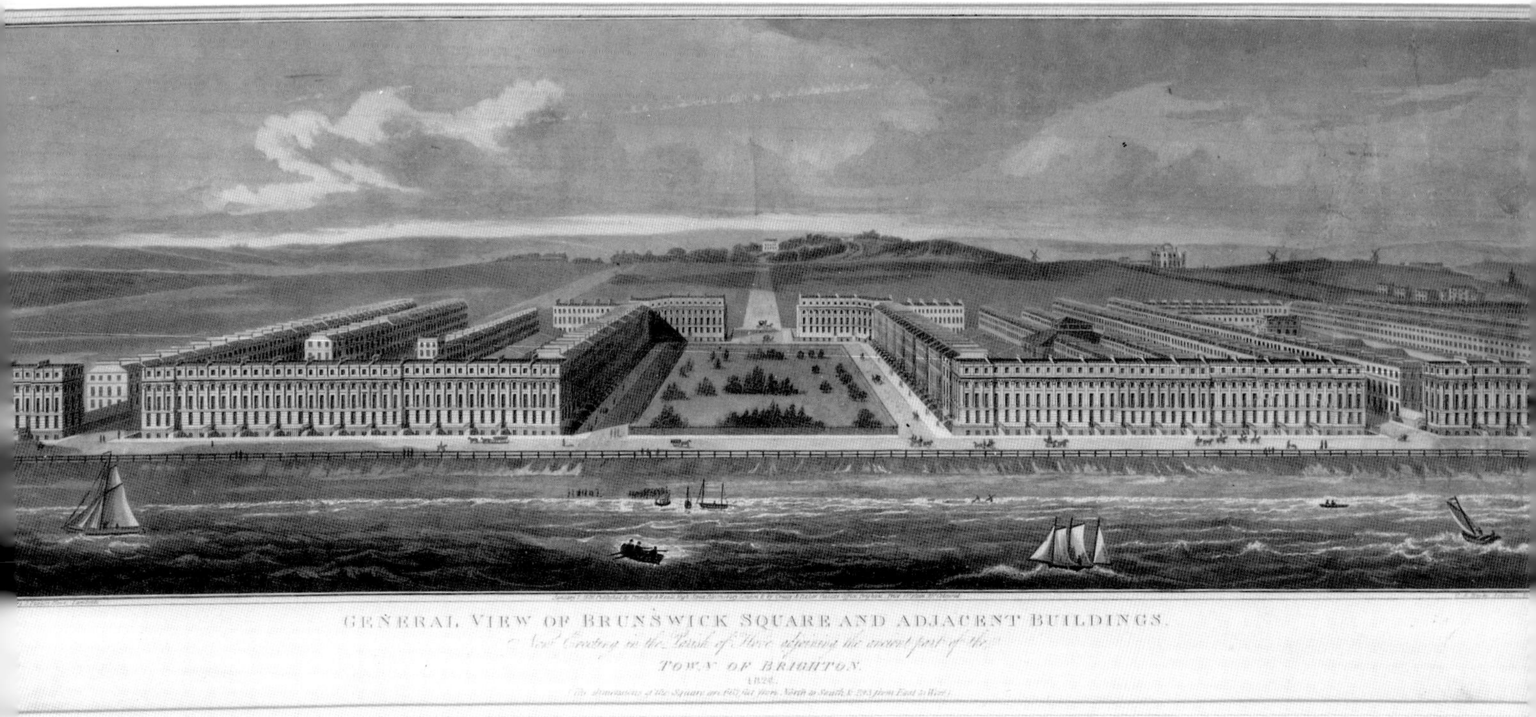

is almost as desolate as Pompeii after its two thousand years' burial."(7) Even with work begun on planting the central gardens, creating the esplanade along the front and erecting railings and lamp standards, purchasers were scarce. Much of Chichester Terrace was not built and dozens of other houses on the estate not completed for several decades. Kemp found himself financially stretched and from 1837 to his death in 1844 he was forced to live abroad.

But back in 1823, soon after he had begun work on Kemp Town and when the market for property in Brighton was rising, Busby too had decided to take a more direct speculative r le. He thus launched his greatest architectural achievement - Brunswick Town.

The landowner for Brunswick Town was the Reverend Thomas Scutt. His property, the Wick Farm Estate, lay just over the boundary line from Brighton in the parish of Hove. Scutt was content to let Busby take not only the designing but the entrepreneurial lead and quickly sold off most of the individual building plots for a handsome profit, although until 1830 when the estate was vested under the authority of a Board of Commissioners, Scutt retained considerable legal control over Brunswick Town.

Busby's plan for Brunswick Town drew superficially upon that for Kemp Town: ranges of terraces of first class houses along the sea with a long square stretching up and back.(8) (Figs.39 & 40) The streets running from Western Road down to the sea were for smaller second class houses, a hotel, a chapel and

40
Brunswick Town, engraved by M. Dubourg, 1826. When this view was printed, only the two long blocks of Brunswick Terrace which flank either side of the Square were nearing completion.

public baths. The service streets behind, as well as containing the usual mews, provided for a large market building and a public house. Along the extended Western Road there were to be shops.

Construction on the first stages of Brunswick Town began around March 1824 and proceeded rapidly.(9) The first sections to be wholly completed, by September 1826, were the two blocks of Brunswick Terrace on either side of the Square.(10) (Fig.41)

The façades of Brunswick Terrace were Busby's most formal architectural designs and provide a compositional link to architecture he had admired in America. At the same time that he was creating the designs for Brunswick Terrace, Busby was also making an etching from his measured drawings of the Capitol Building in Washington. Although by no means a copy, Busby treated the Hove façades in a similar manner. Admittedly, the elevations of the Capitol are based upon English Palladian precedent, making Busby's stylistic reference traditional; yet his design carries similar vertical fenestration with the same arrangement of Corinthian pilasters and columns as the Washington Capitol. With the drawings of the Capitol Building and Brunswick Terrace going through his mind at the same time, it is little wonder that Busby intermingled the designs, even to the point of omitting the ground floor window keystones of the Capitol to bring them in line with those of the Terrace.

Busby designed six houses to the east of these seafront façades which carried their own individuality. Confusingly, this row was still called Brunswick Terrace. (Fig.42) These are very large houses and with their sea views were considered the most desirable to rent for the season.

The first three years of Busby's time in

41
Brunswick Terrace at the southwest corner of Brunswick Square, photographed in the early 1900s. The house in the Square, No. 58 (on the right), was built in 1875, covering a long-standing gap.

Brighton were to be the busiest of his career. As the town enjoyed a building boom, Busby and A.H. Wilds were there to meet its demands. Although the two architects were in partnership during this period, they mostly worked separately. Busby maintained a leading edge over his partner in the number and scale of his commissions. At the time that Kemp and Brunswick Towns were in fledgling states, Busby had taken on two other projects both similar in conception.

42
Nos.1 to 6 Brunswick Terrace.

The first was Portland Place. This was a speculative development by a local resident, Major Villeroy Russell, who owned a strip of seafront property in Brighton just about half way between the town centre and Kemp Town. For Russell's own residence, Busby designed a large domed mansion, Portland House. Its accommodation was lavish: an entrance hall with a staircase; a dining room, 31' x 22' with a vaulted ceiling; a drawing room 30' x 24'; a library; a ladies' sitting room; 22 sleeping, dressing and servants' rooms; and stabling for ten horses and six carriages.(11) The east side of the mansion overlooked Busby's new Chapel of St George; the south side, with its massive six-columned Corinthian portico, looked down the newly created Portland Place to the sea.

Portland Place itself was lined with terraced houses designed by Busby with façade treatments very much in the style of Kemp Town.(12) (Fig.43) The development continued along Marine Parade, to the west, with a terrace of five houses. Busby again employed the same elevation as the Brunswick Terrace fronts, although without pavilion ends or central pediment.

A serious incident almost halted the project. On the night of 12 September 1825, a fire began under the dome of the nearly completed Portland House. Almost the whole structure was destroyed in a spectacular blaze watched by thousands of onlookers up and down the coast, and by residents and visitors who flocked onto the Downs for a better view of what one observer described as "a most imposing *coup-d'oeil*."(13)

Busby's spirits must have sunk at the sight, especially when he discovered that Major Russell carried no insurance. But the Major rallied, and the house was rebuilt virtually as planned, but without the central dome.(14) (Fig.44) By 1828, the street was finished and most of the houses taken.(15) Two years later, Busby exhibited his Portland Place scheme in the Royal Academy Exhibition.(16)

The second, similar project which Busby

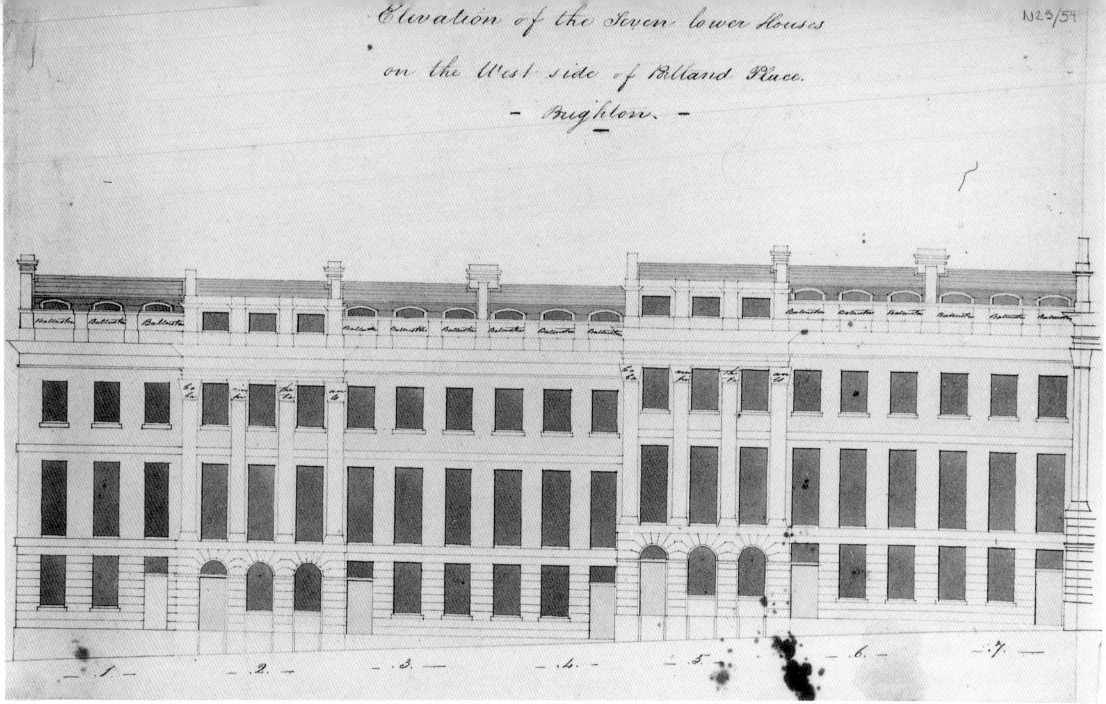

43
Elevation of the west side of Portland Place, *c*1824. The façades are in the style of nearby Kemp Town.

44
Portland Place and Portland House, Brighton. Drawn by F.Forde and engraved by W.J. Alais, *c*1845. Busby designed this development for Major Russell between about 1824 and 1828. Portland House was Busby's most important town house.

45
Design for Cavendish Place, *c*1825. This magnificent 4 foot long drawing, with laid-out elevations and a perspective, was prepared to entice potential buyers.

had in hand at this time was for Cavendish Place (known at first as Cavendish Square) and a large mansion for the landowner. The Count and Countess of St Antonio, amongst the brightest stars to frequent Brighton society, had a house with extensive grounds near Regency Square, on what was called the West Cliff, the coastal stretch lying west of the town centre as far as Brunswick Town. In the early summer of 1825 they sold the contents and materials of the house - from bedsteads to roofing slates - in order to clear the way for their contribution to the local housing boom.(17) They had already asked Busby to draw up the design for the square and their new mansion(18) (Fig.45) and publish a print of the scheme in order to attract potential property buyers.(19)

The Count of St Antonio auctioned off the plots in the square prior to construction. But several did not sell and this might well account for the abandonment of the mansion.(20) The terraces, however, were erected; though the site of the proposed mansion received a large building of much plainer treatment. The square thus lacked its *tour de force*. Matters were made worse in the Victorian period when incongruous bay windows were added to several of the houses to give oblique views of the sea, compensating for Busby's lack of bow fronts.

Successful on the whole as all these building schemes had been, Busby did suffer some disappointments during his first years in Brighton. In the summer of 1823, the new firm of Wilds and Busby entered the competition to find a design for Brighton's largest church to date, St Peter. Their Gothic design was nothing less than Busby's controversial Leeds church, re-drawn to provide a wider nave for a larger congregation.(21) (Fig.46) Wilds and Busby came second out of 79 entries, losing to

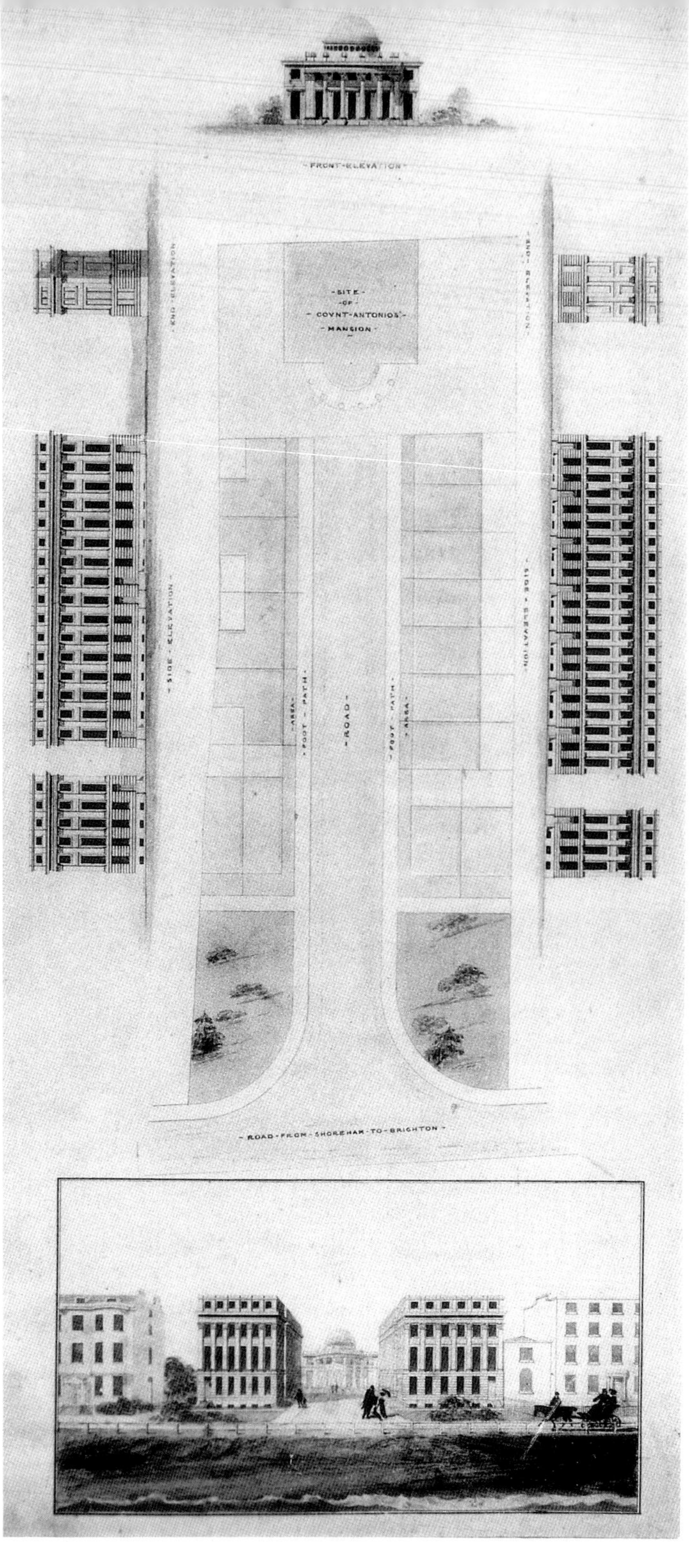

46
Longitudinal section of Wilds & Busby's competition design for the Church of St Peter, Brighton, 1823. The competition was won by Charles Barry.

the then relatively unknown Charles Barry.(22) The St Peter's competition increased Wilds and Busby's prestige. In the local papers, the partners published the same design that Busby had used on the front of his printed diatribe against the Church Commissioners in 1822. And, at their North Lodge office, they exhibited a wooden model of the church, undoubtedly made by Busby, which became a popular attraction.(23)

The young Charles Barry, by no fault of his own, was to block Busby's path on three more occasions. Early in 1824, Busby accompanied the Reverend Edward Everard on a visit to possible sites for a new County Hospital and Sea Bathing Infirmary. A year later, Everard, as Secretary of the hospital building committee, reassured Busby that when the committee next met, the job of architect would be his. But Everard had to bow to the wishes of Lord Egremont, spokesman of the committee, and to Thomas Attree, a prominent local businessman, who favoured another architect, presumably Barry.

Busby was outraged by what he considered an act of betrayal. Never one to take such matters quietly, he attempted to expose the treachery of the hospital committee. He wrote a letter to the *Brighton Gazette*, relating how Everard had shaken his hand and said "Mr Busby you may depend on me," only to discover later that the names of Wilds and Busby had not even been put forward to the committee.(24)

The hospital committee opened the project to architectural competition, which so incensed Busby that he again published his opinion.(25) Barry, however, still won the competition and built the hospital.

In another instance when the paths of Busby and Barry crossed, Busby remained silent, though his pride must have been hurt. Barry was chosen to design the chapel for Brunswick Town. After his public attack on the Reverend Edward Everard it is not surprising that Busby should not be asked to design the chapel of St Andrew in Waterloo Street, where Everard was to be the minister. The site lay just beyond Scutt's property and was thus outside Busby's control. The foundation stone for the chapel of one of Barry's earliest essays in the Italian Revival style was laid in April 1827;(26) the building was consecrated by the Bishop of Chichester on 15 July 1828.(27)

Before the hospital controversy, Busby and Everard had been on friendly terms. Everard, prior to moving to St Andrew's, was minister to the Chapel of St Margaret, Brighton, a church most likely designed by Busby. Opened in December 1824, St Margaret's was a speculative chapel of ease, erected at the expense of Bernard Gregory who hoped to make a profit on the sale of pews;(28) Gregory, the scurrilous editor of the Tory *Brighton Gazette*, went so far as to name the church after his wife Margaret who, having laid the foundation stone, had a poem dedicated to her which began "Hail! sister o' the plummet line".(29)

In the local press reports on the progress of

47
Church of St Margaret Brighton. Busby's finest church was demolished in 1959.

the chapel's construction, neither the name of Busby nor the partnership of Wilds and Busby were mentioned. Messrs Cooper and Lynn, a local architectural firm who also acted as builders, were twice mentioned in the *Brighton Gazette* in connection with the chapel(30), as was a mysterious Mr I. Clarke of London.(31) But a complete set of working drawings for St Margaret's survives (Colour plate VII) and these, although unsigned and not drawn by Busby, have notes on them in his hand which suggests that the church itself is by Busby.

St Margaret's was the climax of Busby's work in the Greek Revival style. (Fig.47) The west elevation, with its strong Ionic portico

48
The Chain Pier Vase, designed by Busby in 1824 and presented to Captain Samuel Brown, engineer of the Chain Pier, Brighton's most popular attraction.

crowned by a tower in the form of the Tower of the Winds, was modelled on the Inwoods' Church of St Pancras in London (1819-22).

Two weeks after the consecration of St Margaret's, Busby won public acknowledgement for a design that was not for a building. On 13 January 1825, the shareholders of the Chain Pier Company, with their chairman Thomas Read Kemp, gathered for dinner at the Old Ship Hotel to thank Captain Samuel Brown for constructing the Pier. In the two years that it had been open, thousands of residents and visitors had paid a small fee to promenade along its length. It was a financial as well as a popular success. On the evening of the dinner, Brown was presented with a reward for his services, the Chain Pier Vase, which had been designed by Busby.(32) (Fig.48)

The Chain Pier Vase is a large covered cup, made of silver, with a capacity of two gallons. Standing 25 inches in height and with a circumference of 18 inches, it weighs 27 1/2 pounds. The cover is adorned by the figure of a seated Britannia, a trident in one hand, a lion at her side. Encircling the body of the vase is an embossed view of the Chain Pier with a scene of ships and sailboats by the artist George Chinnery. Appropriately, two large anchors form the handles, joined around the top by chain cables. For feet, Busby chose the Arms of Brighton, a trio of dolphins.

Busby's other non-architectural piece of design from about this period was for a gothic bookcase made for the Reverend Doctor Samuel Holland, Prebendary of Chichester Cathedral and Rector of Poynings in Sussex.(33) (Colour plate VIII)

The rebuilding of Union Street Chapel, in the Brighton Lanes, might have been a close collaboration between Wilds and Busby. When tenders were announced in March 1825, the plans were available for inspection at their office,(34) and the designs attributed to both architects.(35) However, a surviving plan and elevation of the chapel, although not signed, is another example of Busby's fine draughtsmanship. (Fig.49) But when Union Street Chapel opened in August 1825, after Wilds and Busby had dissolved their partnership, Wilds's name was alone connected to the work.(36)

Certain buildings which came under the umbrella of Wilds and Busby would have suited the temperament of one partner more

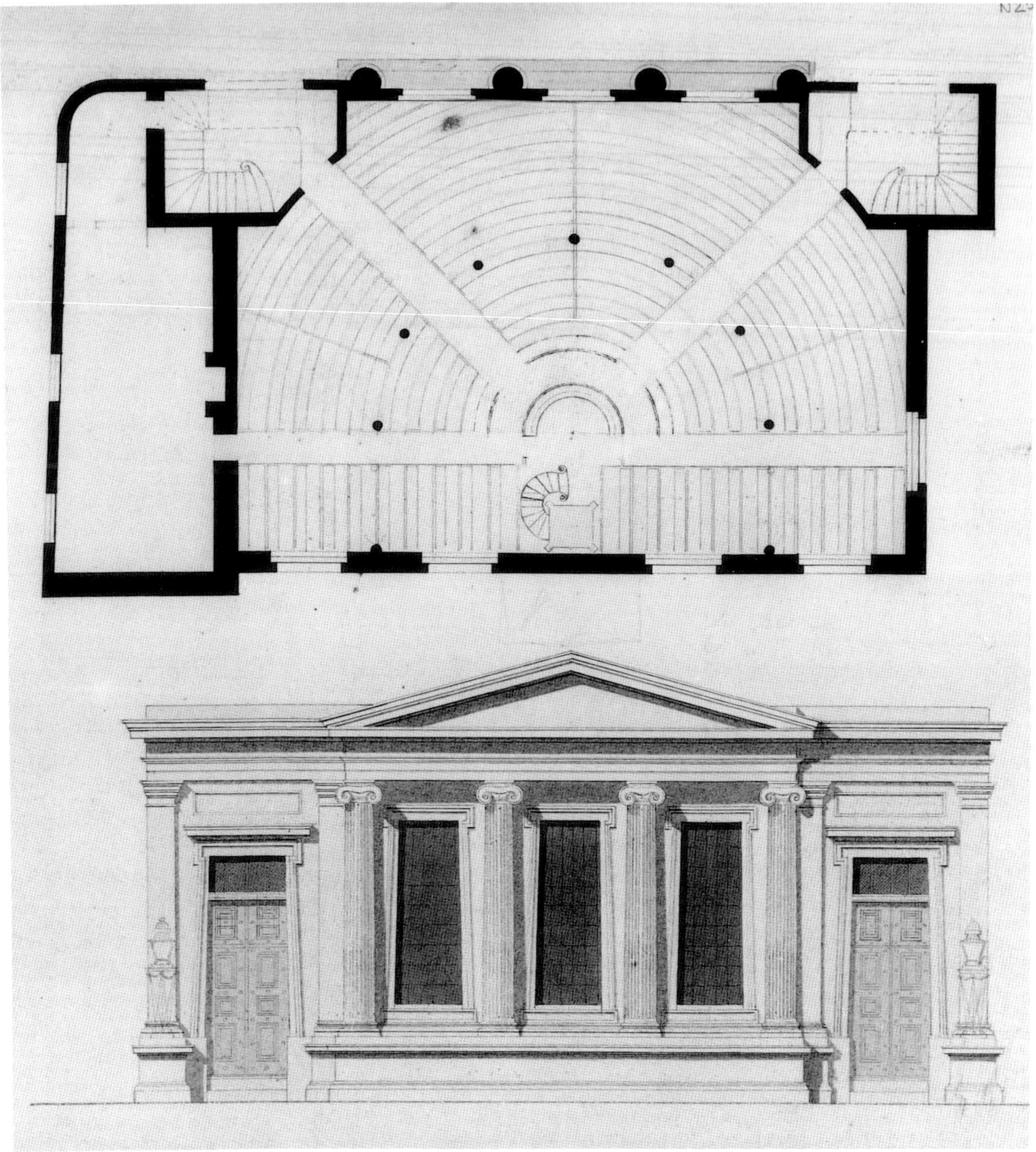

49
Plan and elevation of the Union Street Chapel, c1825. A drawing by Busby of a chapel by his partner Amon Henry Wilds.

than the other. When it was announced in April 1825 that Wilds and Busby were to erect a bathing establishment in Kemp Town for Sake Deen Mahomed, "Shampooing Surgeon

50
The ammonite capital and scallop shell, such as these in Oriental Place, Brighton, are the hallmarks of buildings designed by Amon Henry Wilds.

to His Majesty King George IV", and that "the style of architecture will be in strict accordance with the purest examples of Indian composition," such a commission would have suited Wilds.(37) A.H. Wilds, with the same sense of humour that had led him to adopt the ammonite capital, enjoyed extending the exoticism of the Royal Pavilion in his Brighton architecture. During the late 1820s he built his own house, the Western Pavilion - which in name and miniature appearance aped the King's palace - as well as Sillwood Place, with windows in the shape of cusped pointed arches found in Islamic architecture.

Wilds and Busby designed and altered dozens of buildings in Brighton. In many cases documentary evidence is thin or nonexistent, leaving attribution to be made on stylistic grounds. The ammonite capital and scallop shell are the hallmarks of an A.H. Wilds building (Fig.50) in much the same way as a Busby terrace house can be readily identified by its proportion, fenestration and use of the orders. An excellent example of a Busby residence, although no written proof exists to show it as such, is Chichester House, standing at the end of Chichester Terrace.(38) (Fig.51)

Relations between the two architects were by no means harmonious. The partnership had been a marriage of convenience based on the commission for Kemp Town. As the leading partner, it annoyed Busby to have all his work linked to someone who had little or nothing to do with his designs. Even commissions taken on before moving to Brighton had now to be shared under the formal arrangements of partnership. For example, when the first stone for Busby's chapel in Maidenhead was laid, on 22 July 1824, both architects attended and the church was assigned to Wilds and Busby.(39)

The last straw for Busby was Brunswick Town. In 1825, at the Royal Academy Exhibition, the partners submitted two large architectural perspectives. One was of Kemp Town, and was listed in the catalogue as being by "Wilds and Busby", the legal name of the partership.(40) The other perspective was of Brunswick Town, and bore the exhibiting names of "Busby and Wilds".(41) This is the only written instance in which Busby's name was placed before Wilds's.

No longer able to work together, Amon Henry Wilds and Charles Augustin Busby dissolved their partnership on 24 June 1825.(42) As their solicitor said afterwards: "When it was executed there was much difference between the parties."(43)

Busby now felt very possessive about the authorship of his designs. After the dissolution of partnership, he systematically scratched out Wilds's name on all drawings which were his design alone. So although originally signed by both architects, such drawings for example

51
Chichester House, Kemp Town, Brighton.

as the gothic bookcase and a design for a house made in August 1823 for Mr R. Newnham,(44) had Wilds's name removed.

Wilds, now on his own, prospered. His style matured and many of Brighton's finest buildings are his, including the Albion Hotel, the Royal Newburgh Assembly Rooms, the Victoria fountain in the Steine and the very beautiful Montpelier Crescent. A.H. Wilds also worked outside Brighton, designing a country house for Sir Aubrey Hunter near Limerick in Ireland, and a villa for the Earl of Onslow, near West Clandon.(45) The town hall at Gravesend, Kent is also Wilds's.

Busby and his family remained at 13 Waterloo Place, which he now also used as his office. One of his first independent jobs was to design Cranbourne Street, a short thoroughfare with 18 shops between West Street and Grenville Place.(46)

On a grander scale was Busby's attempt to build along the coast west from Brunswick Town. Again, he came up against Charles Barry's growing popularity in Brighton. The large property owner for this area of Hove was William Stanford. Seizing upon Brighton's seaside building fever, Stanford asked both Busby and Barry to draw up schemes for estates in the manner of Kemp and Brunswick Towns. Barry, who was probably approached first, produced a series of drawings in October 1825 for an estate comparable to Brunswick Town in its amenities: a series of residential squares centred on a market building.(47) But

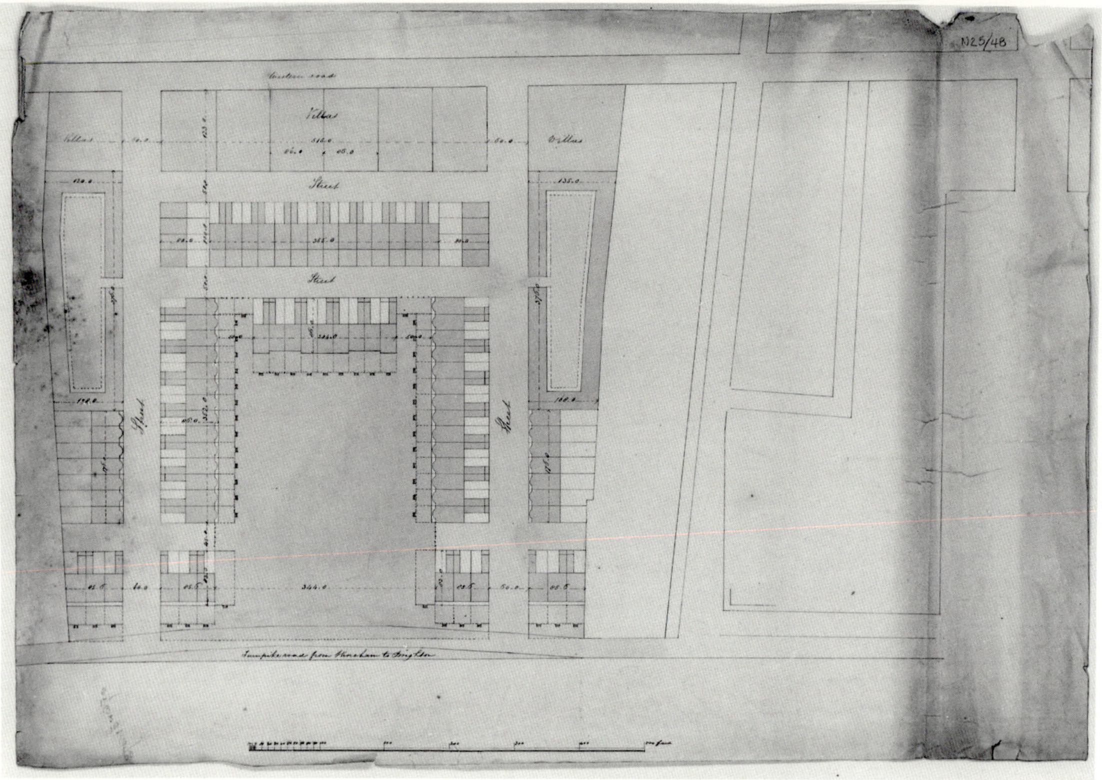

52
Plan for the Stanford Estate, *c*1826. A scheme by Busby to extend Brunswick Town along the coast to the west.

Barry's development lacked a sense of sweeping grandeur necessary to the site. Busby's proposal, probably produced in 1826 or '27, was more economical than Barry's, consisting of a simple open square of terraced houses facing the sea and a row of villas on the Western Road.(48) (Fig.52) In the event, neither scheme was chosen by Stanford.

About 1825-26, Busby made a seductive design for a set of terrace houses which, sadly, were not executed.(49) (Fig.53) The terraces may have borne some relation to the Stanford Estate, although the scale relates to nothing in Busby's scheme, especially the 95 foot wide street which divides the set of houses. Destined for "the West Cliff", they were most likely prepared for a virgin plot somewhere just east of Brunswick Terrace.

Would the façades of another of Busby's unexecuted schemes - a semicircular crescent of houses - have been as beautiful? As only the ground floor plan survives, little clue is given.(50) (Fig.54)

Work was well advanced upon the first stages of Brunswick Terrace when Busby and Wilds went their separate ways in the summer of 1825. Not long afterwards, Busby published a large plan of the western part of Brighton "shewing the magnificent building arrangements now in rapid progress in the adjoining Parish of Hove".(51) (Fig.55) Busby, whose name appears as sole architect at the

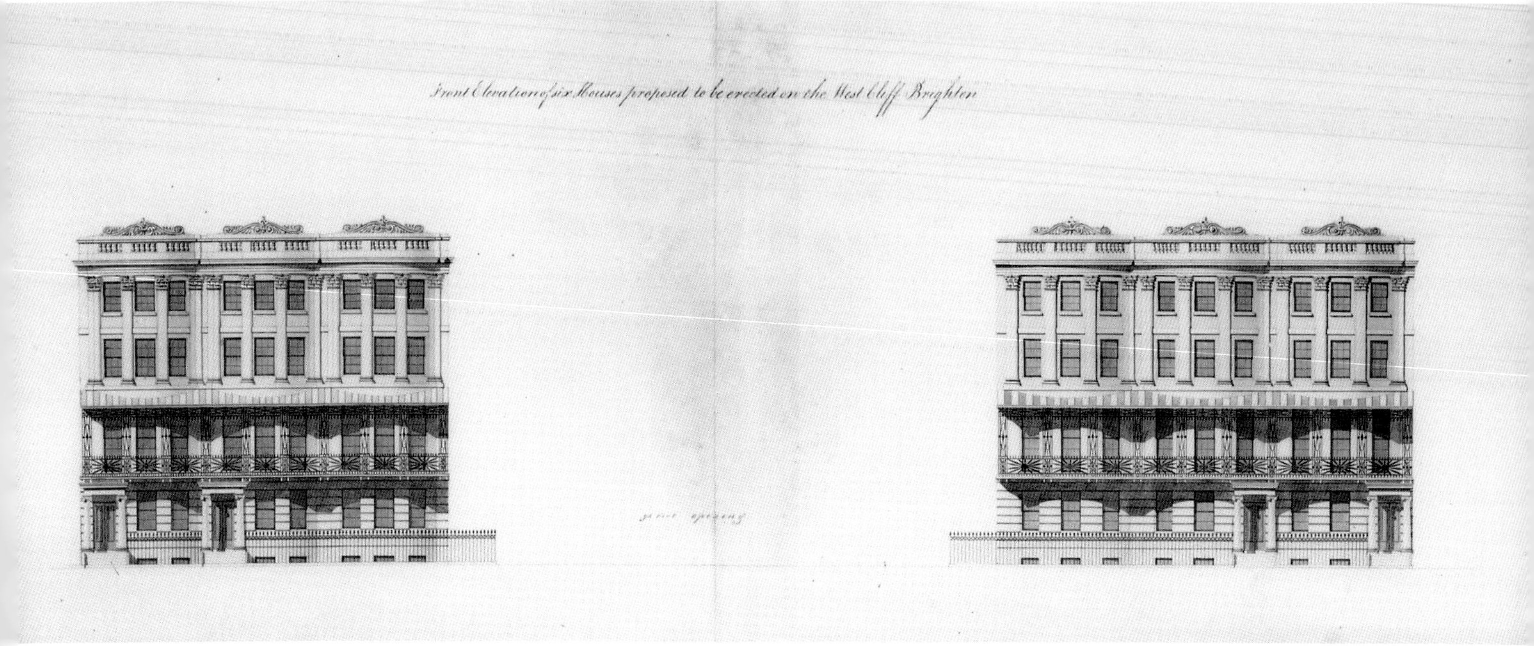

bottom of the sheet, also highlighted Cavendish Place.

At the end of 1824, Busby had begun to finalize the upper part of Brunswick Square, at its opening into the Western Road, by laying out building plots for shops and houses.(52) As his initial idea for a small thoroughfare failed to give adequate depth to the buildings, Busby resolved upon creating a small access avenue called Brunswick Place.(53)

The eight bow fronted houses on Brunswick Place were completed by March 1828, at which time the residents petitioned for the laying of street pavements and erection of gas lamp standards.(54) At one point during the design stage, Busby contemplated having a ballroom along the east side of Brunswick Place.(55) (Figs.56 & 57) The southern house, No.8, was retained in the scheme, but integrated so as to form additional accommodation for guests and management. The ballroom itself would have been a grand space, 50 feet long and 40 feet wide, with an arched ceiling 30 feet high. Busby had clear ideas about the internal decoration, noting that "the walls to be painted 4 times in oil colours, & laid out in pannels or distemper to correspond."

The plots in Brunswick Town were bought mainly by local builders, merchants, solicitors

53
Unexecuted design for six houses on the West Cliff, Brighton, *c*1825. The houses were most likely destined for the area around Cavendish Square.

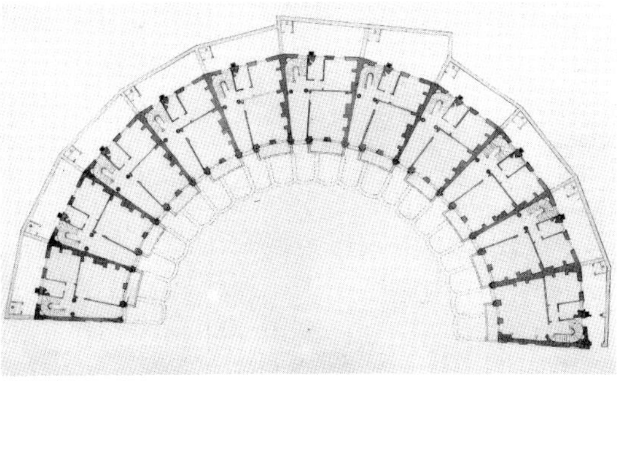

54
Unexecuted design for a crescent of terrace houses, *c*1827.

55
Plan of Brunswick Town and adjacent Brighton streets, printed in 1825.

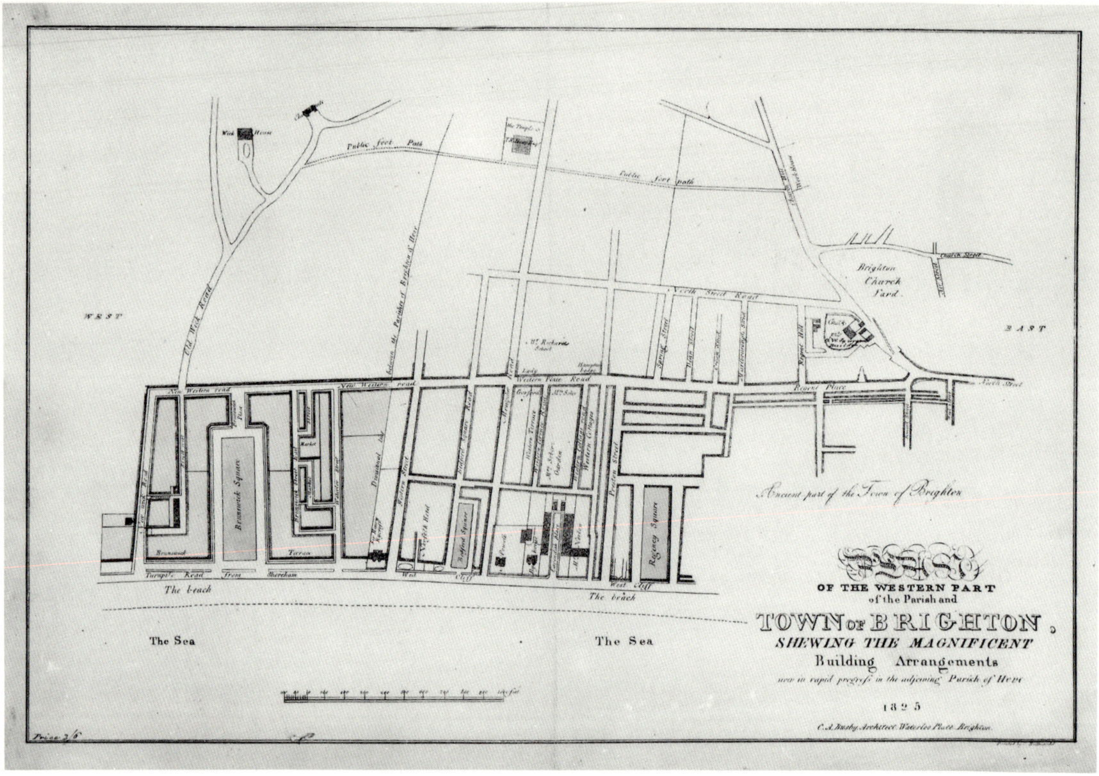

and gentlemen. The purchaser was obliged to enter into contract with the landowner, the Reverend Scutt, the architect, Busby, and the individual builder. Often, the more wealthy purchasers bought stretches of adjacent plots; for example, Charles Elliott and Busby's friend Jacob Boys between them attempted to purchase most of the north-east side of the Square.(56) After the houses were erected, many of the developers sold their properties for a quick profit.(57) In 1827 there were less than a dozen landowners in the parish of Hove; by 1830 this figure had risen to 60, almost all concentrated in Brunswick Town.(58) Hove was a good parish to buy in, for as the advertisements for Brunswick Town stressed, residents escaped the payment of three shillings per cauldron on coals plus the heavier tax and poor rates of Brighton.(59)

Although a compositional and visual whole, Busby designed Brunswick Square in a ranked series of differing blocks: at each change of roof level, the façade is almost always treated in a different manner. But for a few variations in detail and plot size, the west side of Brunswick Square is almost a mirror image of the east side. (Colour plate IX, Figs.58 & 59) Along the top of the square (Colour plates X & XI), Busby reverted to his favourite Brunswick Terrace and Cavendish Place façade design, with the variant of a semicircular moulding over the square inset window in the attic

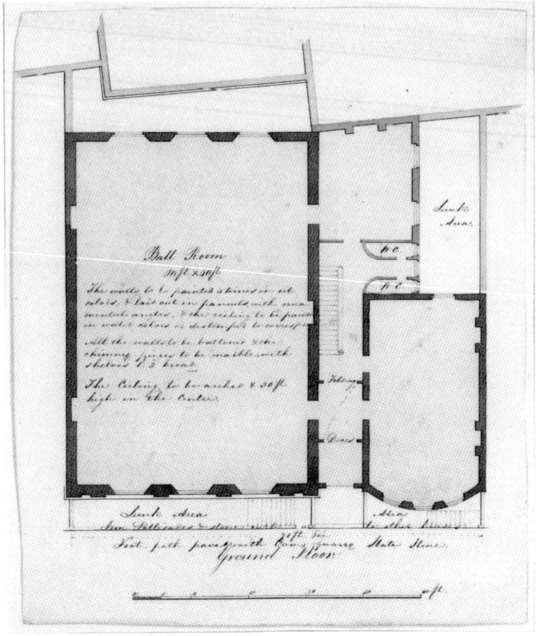

56
Plan for a ballroom and No.8 Brunswick Place, Hove, c1827.

57
Elevation for a ballroom and No.8 Brunswick Place, Hove, *c*1827. Only the house was built.

58
Nos.52 (on the right) & 54 Brunswick Square. No.52 is one of four similar houses in the Square which, contrary to popular opinion, is contemporary with its neighbours and is not a later infill.

storey.(60) The two exceptions to the symmetry are the two houses which face one another across the square: No.1 is a single house with a double bay, one with Corinthian columns, the other without; and No.58, the last house in the square, at the south-east corner, which was not built until about 1875.(61) Its sympathetic front, with a central doorway flanked by asymetrical bays, covered a long-standing gap.

Most of the houses in Brunswick Square and Brunswick Place vary in size and even within a group of similar houses widths often differ. The basic layout of the interiors are like those for Kemp Town and was based on a typical 18th century formula plan of first class town houses. Entrances, often with porticos, were to one side of the house front. Having entered, the staircase lay straight ahead at the end of the hall. The basement contained the servants' quarters of kitchen, scullery, pantry, wine cellars, and shoe and knife closets; a back door gave access to a yard and outside privy, and in some cases led to the coach house and stables. Often there was a housekeeper's room near the front of the basement. Coal and beer were stored in vaults under the pavement. Above, at the front on the ground floor was the dining room. The parlour or morning room

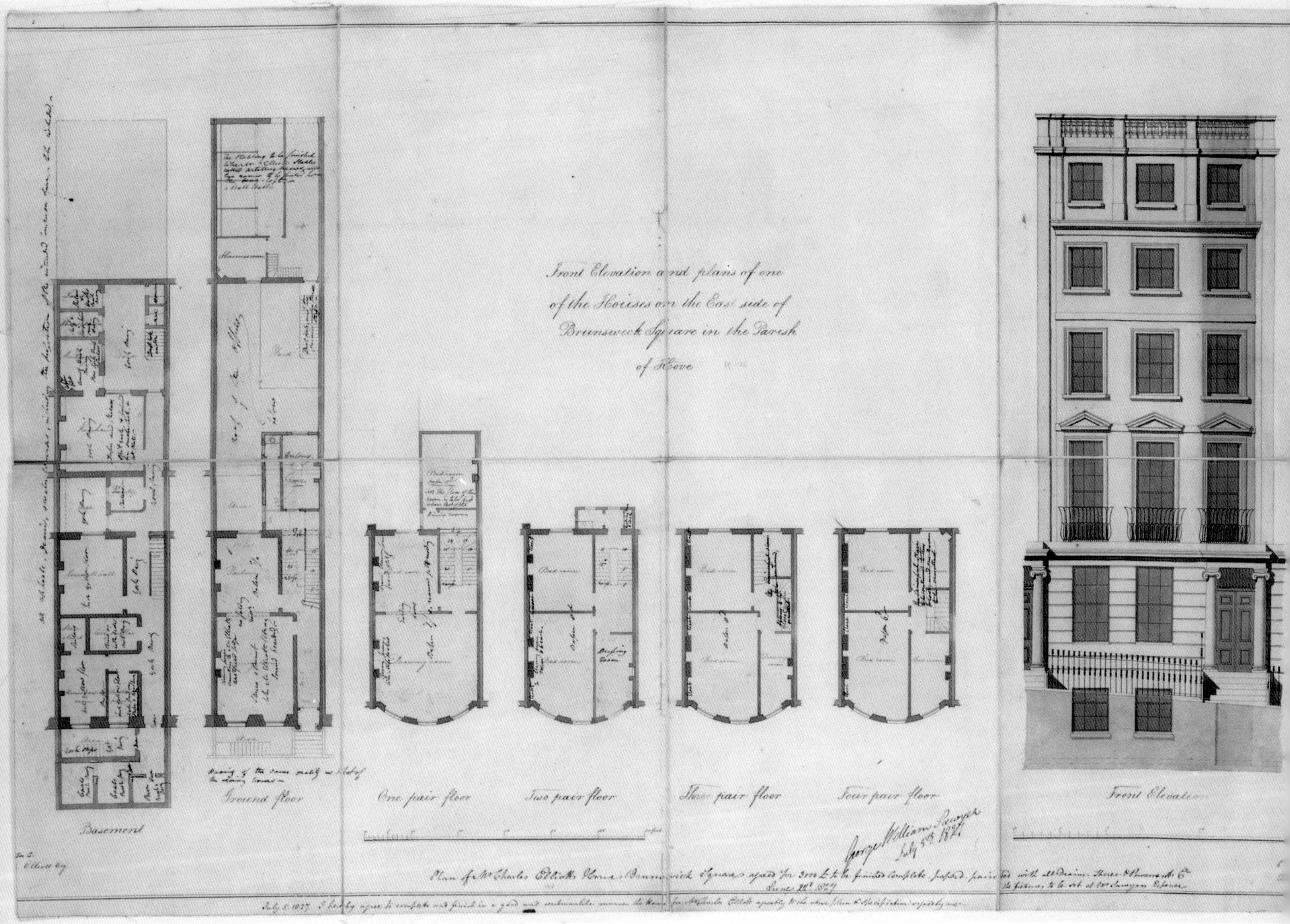

59
Presentation drawing for No.19 Brunswick Square, almost as built, 1827.

lay behind and might either be entered off the hall or directly from the dining room, perhaps through a wide opening flanked by columns or through folding doors. A waiting room and water-closet were common on the half landing that led up to the first floor drawing rooms. Bedrooms occupied the top three storeys. Larger houses had more anti-rooms and water-closets and, at the back, a servants' staircase from the kitchen to the second floor.

The interior decoration of houses in Brunswick Town also varied. As with Kemp

60
Capital, frieze and cornice in the dining room of No.13 Brunswick Square.

Town, the internal finishings were left to the builder and client. All principal rooms were ornamented with rich plaster cornices and marble chimneypieces, (Fig.60) and the principal staircases had decorative iron balusters. Busby may have designed the cornices in some of the houses; other elements were bought. In some instances, outside architects may have made a contribution. George Basevi, father of the architect of the same name, was one of the first residents of Brunswick Square, and may have asked his son to design the interior of his house at No.37.(62) Captain Richard Heaviside hired the young John Gregory Crace to undertake the decoration of his residence at No.15. Crace produced a design for a niche, to contain a large sculpture of Diana the Huntress, set in marblised gold and green side panels of diamond shapes on an ornamented dado.(63) (Fig.61) Marbling and graining were both favourite wall decorations; an 1829 advertisement for the sale of 43 Brunswick Square highlighted the neat papering and painting of the two drawing rooms on the first floor in imitation of satinwood, and in imitation of oak throughout the dining and morning rooms on the ground floor.(64)

The newly built Western Road out of Brighton had reached the northern boundary

61
Design for a niche and wall decoration for Captain Heaviside at No.15 Brunswick Square by John Gregory Crace, *c*1828.

of Brunswick Town by the summer of 1825.(65) A row of shops on the south side of the new road between Brunswick Street East and Brunswick Place was then built to serve the new estate. Busby hesitated over placing shops on the site which he called Brunswick Row,

62
Working drawing for stabling in Regency Mews, Brighton, 1827.

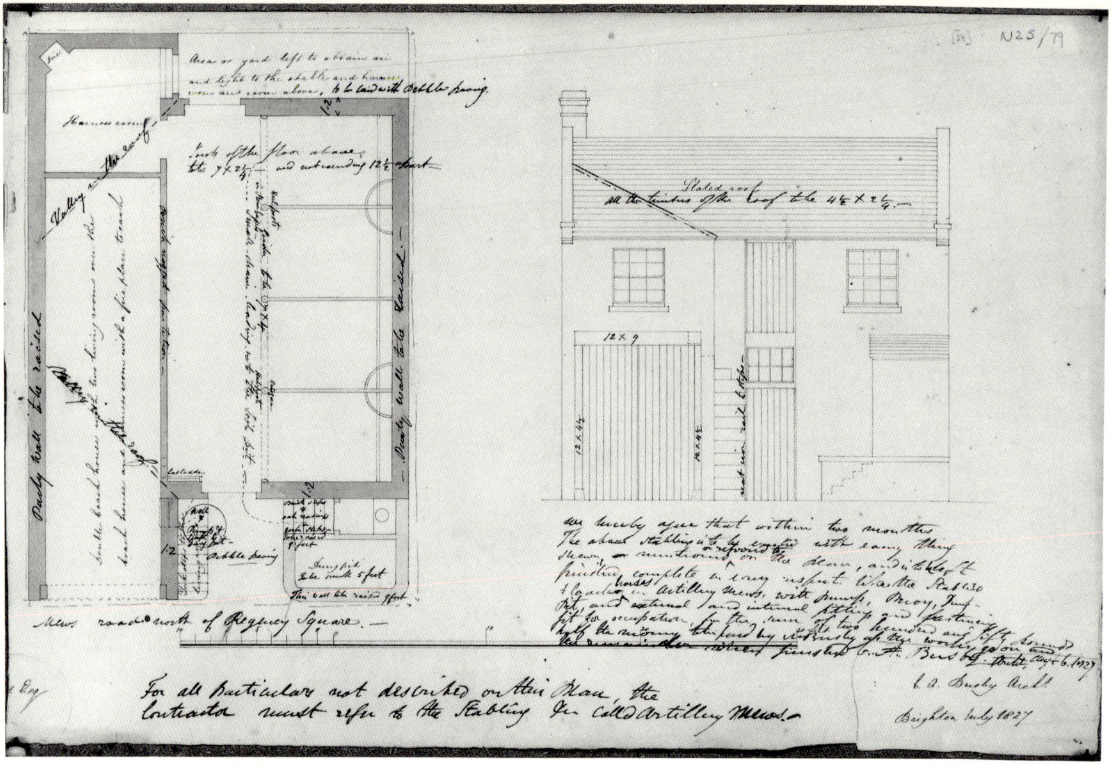

63
Design for the Star of Brunswick Public House, as built, Brunswick Street West, *c*1824.

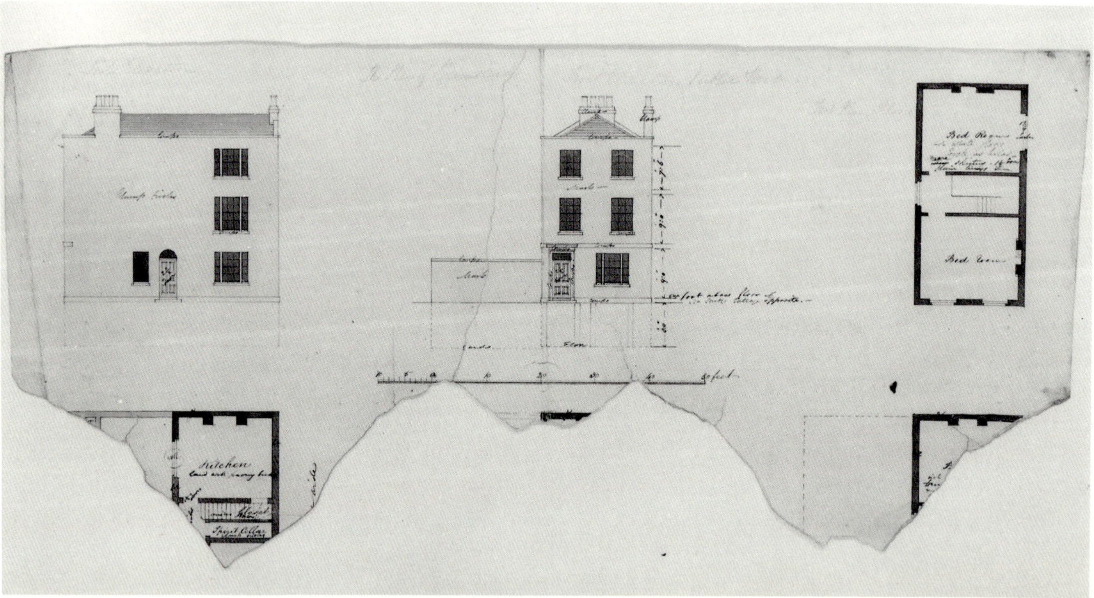

and at first produced a design giving the builder the option of either inserting shop windows and doors on the ground floor, or substituting them for windows and doors for private houses.(66)

Busby had designed shops previous to these. For example, in March 1825 he completed a drawing for a bakery.(67) But this was very utilitarian in comparison to his design for a shop front almost wholly of glass and iron.(68) (Colour plate XII) Busby, in an experimental mood, clad the whole shop front with large window panes fixed by iron mullions with screwed joints. This was a novel innovation. Iron colonettes flank the door and corners of the shop while the ornately patterned grating, balcony and frieze are similar to designs in Busby's early book *Decorative Embellishments*.

The design of the service streets behind Brunswick Square also occupied Busby. Brunswick Street East and Brunswick Street West were narrow alleys of stabling, with cramped living quarters for the coachmen on the first floor.(69) (Fig.62) In Brunswick Street West, Busby built the Star of Brunswick public house, a welcome escape for the local servants.(70) (Fig.63)

A financial panic in Britain beginning in the last months of 1825 marked a gradual decline in Brighton's property boom. By the end of 1826, the local building slump became the subject of a poem, with Kemp Town alluded to as a desert:

"What tho' her career be check'd for awhile,
Yet her strength revive, and the *desert shall smile*."(71)

This downturn in the economy accounted for Busby's difficulty in making a success of his market building.(72) In the spring of 1826 he built a covered market, 100 feet long by 40 feet wide, between Brunswick Street East and Waterloo Street, approached on the north and south by a small access road lined with cheap housing.(73) (Fig.64) It would appear to have been a personal investment. Few tradesmen, however, contacted Busby. For a limited period he attempted to entice vendors by allowing them to rent stalls at the new market for free.(74) But even this proved a failure. As it was, the building did not open until August 1828, and was so unsuccessful that it was soon converted into a riding school.(75)

Despite the economic slump, people continued to flock to Brighton for the season. Every day, the long lists of names printed in the local newspapers were studied to see who had arrived in town, where they were staying, which houses they had rented, who had given a ball or dinner, who had attended and what they had worn. Brunswick Town, especially the Terrace, was now part of the social circuit. During the winter of 1828-29, for example, Brunswick Terrace was home to the Duke and Duchess of Bedford, the Duke and Duchess of St Albans, and the Dowager Duchess of Roxburgh.(76)

Dr Busby's visit to his son in May 1827 was remarked upon in the "Fashionable Chronicle"

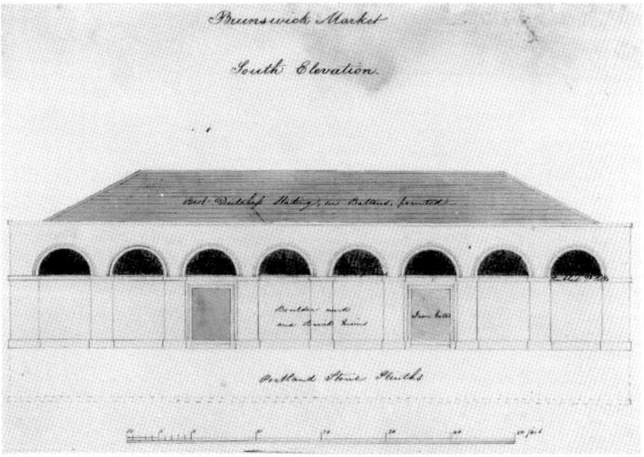

64
Elevation of Brunswick Market, *c*1826. Busby invested in the building of the market.

of the *Brighton Gazette*,(77) and it wasnoted that Charles's brother, Julian, recently had been called to the bar in Lincoln's Inn.(78)

A few weeks previous to Dr Busby's visit, C.A. Busby had been drawn into unfavourable local prominence. His former partner, Amon Henry Wilds, was sued by a former client, Mrs Dulany, for £6000 damages as compensation for neglecting the superintendence of repairs to her house on Grand Parade. The repairs had taken place when Wilds and Busby were still partners; but as Busby explained when called as a witness during the case held at the Sussex Lent Assizes Crown Court in Lewes, the elder Wilds had recommended his son to Mrs Dulany and Busby had not interfered.(79) But the case turned on a legal point, and the court ruled that as the partnership was legally binding, the case would have to be re-heard with the prosecution suing both Wilds and Busby. When the case went to a re-trial in August, the affair had excited so much interest that a crowd travelled to Lewes to hear it. They were greatly disappointed when the matter went to arbitration.(80)

65
Elevation, as built, of No.1 Lansdowne Place, Hove, 1827.

Busby pushed on with his designs for completing Brunswick Town. Although by mid-1827 most of Brunswick Square had been finished, with the central garden planted and the esplanade from Brighton extended to its boundary, the western edge of the estate was still open field.(81) Only the Wick Road cut through this area, leading down to the shore from the Wick Farm, a half mile inland. Busby personally invested heavily in this section of the building works, borrowing principally from his friend Jacob Boys and the London timber merchants Isaac Solly and Sons of St Mary Axe.(82)

From late 1827, Busby began working concurrently on the fourth wing of Brunswick Terrace and a series of houses at the lower end of Wick Road.(83) The foundations were laid before Busby had even completed the designs.(84) The most western block of Brunswick Terrace consists of ten residences and a hotel.(85) The frontage was treated much as its neighbour, but without central and end pavilions, or individual balconies.

Around the corner, on the west side of Wick Road, Busby built a row of four houses called Lansdowne Place. No.1 has the largest front with its entrance centred between a pair of five-storey bows; it is a house deceptively small interior for such a large façade, with a depth half its street length.(86) (Fig.65) The

three adjacent houses form a triple set of bow fronts, with each doorway guarded by a pair of bearded hermes. (Fig.66) Across the road, on the east side and a little to the north beyond a garden, was Stanhope Place, a series of bow fronted houses, plainly treated.(87) (Figs.67 & 68) The most southerly of these, No.1 (now renumbered and re-named 2 Lansdowne Place when in 1834 the Wick Road assumed its present name) was Busby's new residence.(88) (Fig.69) The appellation of 'Stanhope' was a reference to Lord Stanhope, who had investigated Busby's lock designs for the Regent's Canal and after whom Busby had named his son.

At about this same time Busby borrowed

66
The herms at the entrance to No.5 Lansdowne Place.

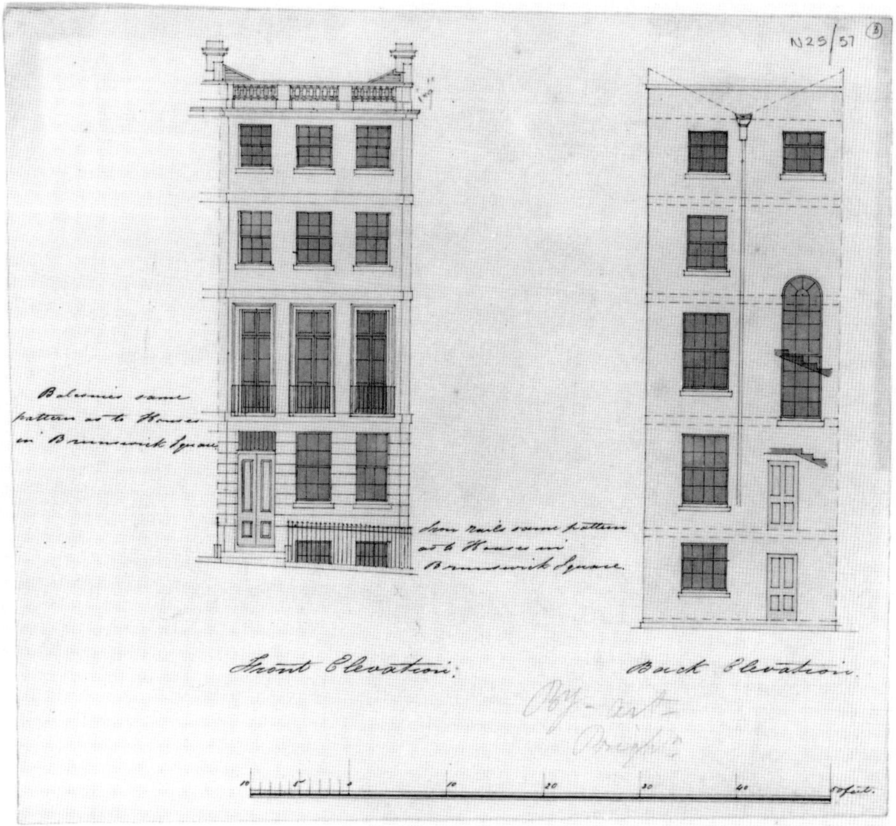

67
Front and rear elevations to a house in Stanhope Place, now Lansdowne Place, *c*1830. This may be Busby's own residence at No.2.

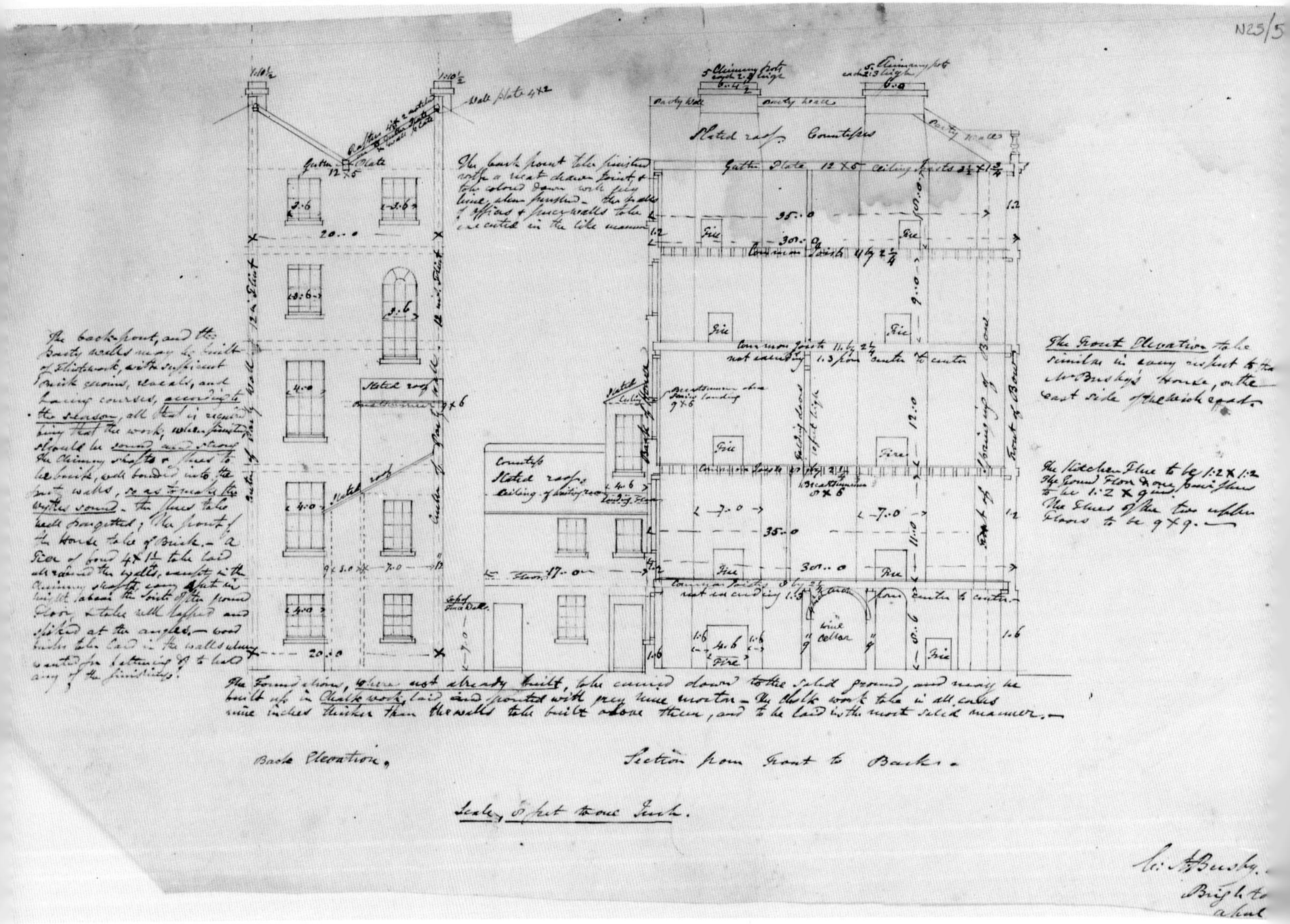

heavily on a speculative development he had undertaken behind Cavendish Place. This was for a row of 13 very small terrace houses that were completed by July 1828: 1-13 Western Buildings, Sobers Gardens, now re-named and re-numbered 13-25 Sillwood Road.(89)

Busby had caught the property investment fever. Slowly, but steadily, he began to overextend himself. When on Christmas Day 1827 he rented a field north of the Western

Road in the Hedgfurlong (the eventual site of Norfolk Road and Borough Street, Brighton) from T.R. Kemp, he was already paying Kemp for a lease on vacant property on Montpelier Road.(90)

Nor did his building ambition stop there. Busby now produced his final scheme for finishing Brunswick Town.(91) (Fig.70) Along the western side of Wick Road, north of Lansdowne Place, he planned large semi-detached villas, set in pairs and spaced between three small squares of lawns and houses. The Western Road was to be extended and lined with houses. And on the extreme west of the estate there was to be a new road leading up from the sea, with 40 terrace houses.

Only a few weeks prior to committing himself to such large financial undertakings, Busby had finally felt solvent enough to return the 40 dollars he had borrowed from Colonel Trumbull nearly a decade previously. He wrote to his old friend on 19 November 1827, remembering the kindness Trumbull and his wife had shown him, and related how he was now "proceeding in a way which bids fair to place [me] far above the frowns of the world, so far at least as property can make a man happy." Trumbull undoubtedly had been to Brighton in the old days, but Busby was pleased to report that the town had "arrived at a degree of splendour which would certainly surprise you. It has been very good fortune to be concerned in *almost all* the large undertakings in the place, and I have profited accordingly. Building ground here, has risen vastly in value, and by a fortunate purchase at the commencement I have already realized a moderate independence."(92)

In the last week of 1829, and during one of the coldest winters in living memory, Busby and his family moved into Stanhope Place.(93) It was a strategic move. The management of Brunswick Town was about to change, and as a substantial property owner and resident, Busby wanted a greater voice in its running.

Under the Brunswick Square (Brighton) Improvement Act, sanctioned on 8 April 1830, Scutt relinquished his control over the estate to a board of Commissioners.(94) These Commissioners, of whom Busby was one, met regularly to discuss the many problems associated with running Brunswick Town.(95) Their responsibilites included the upkeep of the garden, the overseeing of security, drainage, lighting, paving and rate collection. The Commissioners were vigilant over the controls

68
Working drawing for a house in the Wick Road, now Lansdowne Place, *c*1830. The builder is instructed to make the front elevation "similar in every respect to Mr. Busby's House on the east side of the Wick Road."

69
Nos. 2 & 4 Lansdowne Place, formerly Nos. 1 & 2 Stanhope Place, Wick Road, Hove. Busby lived in the house on the right.

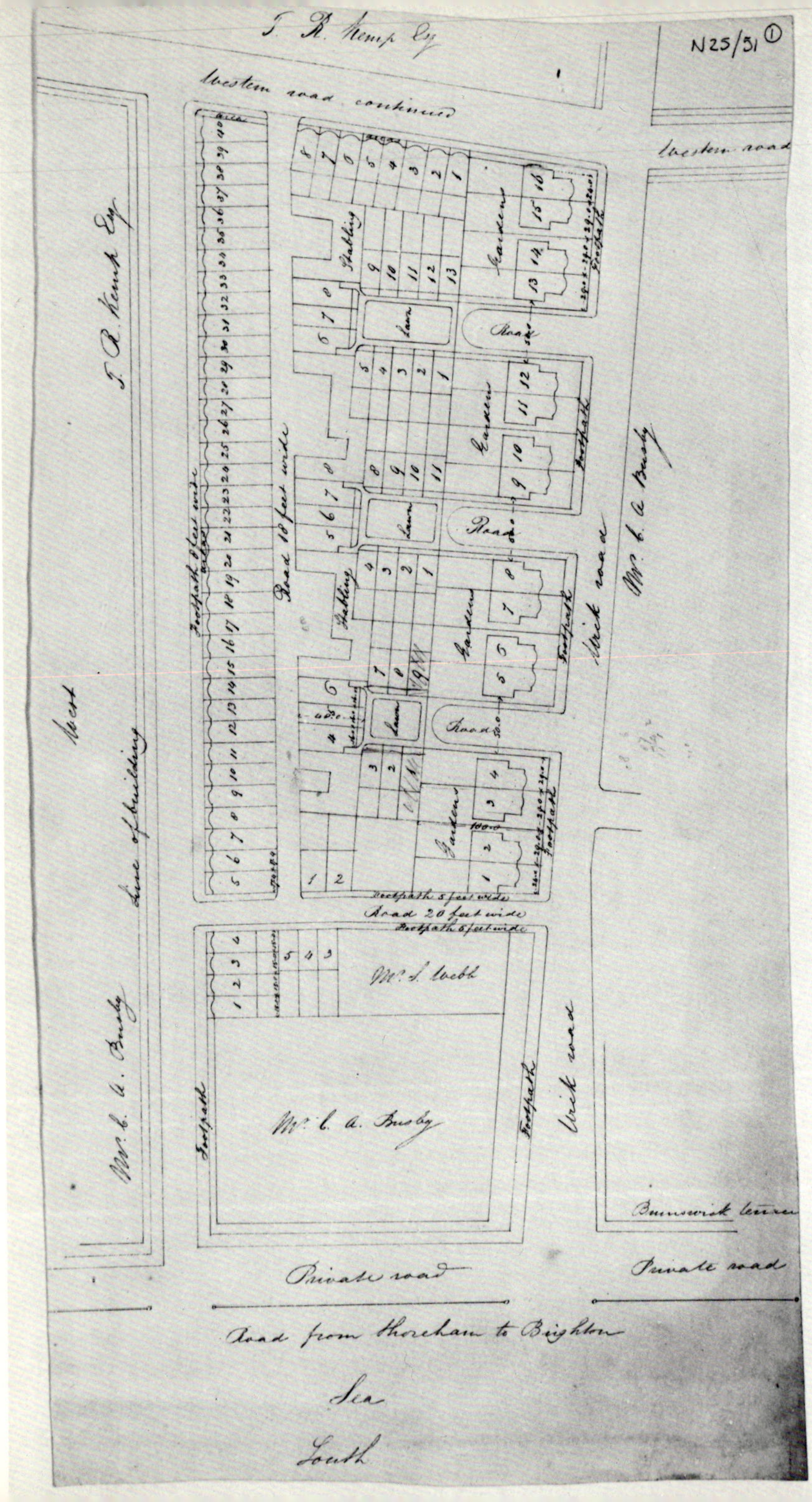

placed upon façade maintenance: exteriors were to remain covered in "Parker's or Roman Cement" and painted every three years in a prescribed colour. No deviations in pattern from the existing balconies or iron railings were allowed.

Busby sold the Commissioners a plot of land he owned on Brunswick Street West for the erection of a fire station. The surveyor to the estate, Thomas Weston Clisby, was responsible for the building's design.(96)

T.W. Clisby had served as clerk to Wilds and Busby, and as such had even been examined in the Dulany court case.(97) After the break-up of the partnership, Clisby probably remained under Busby's direction in some capacity, perhaps helping with the drawings for Brunswick Town. He was the logical choice for estate surveyor. But he too became involved in property speculation, with disastrous consequences. At a meeting of the Commissioners on 9 July 1832, Busby reported that Clisby had sailed for America.(98) Facing bankruptcy, he had fled.(99) Meanwhile, Busby took up the post of surveyor to the Brunswick Estate.

The first years of William IV's reign coincided with a period of strong social and political fervour centred around the reform of the parliamentary electoral system. The landowners, businessmen and professional classes of Brighton were predominantly Whig supporters, in favour of a greater representation by the people. The town had grown, but still only maintained a small voice in Parliament. The Brighton Commissioners and Vestry took every opportunity to solicit the King and Government with strongly worded petitions on issues of the day.(100)

As the first stage of the Reform Bill made its way through Parliament, Busby threw

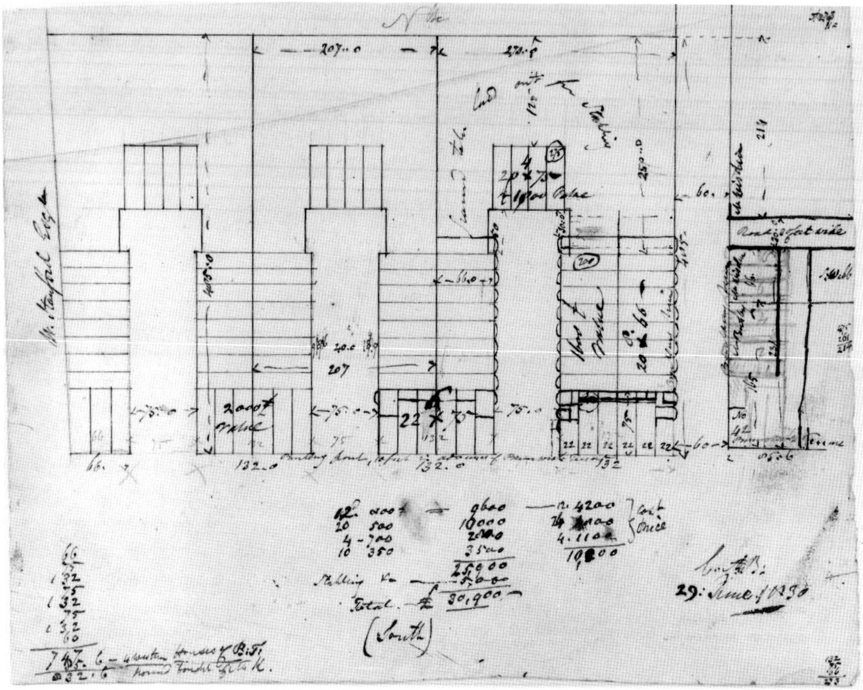

70
Unexecuted plan for completing the development of the Wick Road area, now Lansdowne Place, Hove, *c*1827. Only Lansdowne Square, the southern of the three proposed squares, was built.

71
Unexecuted plan for three squares on the "Adelaide Crescent" site, Hove, 1830. Busby's second attempt at building on the site.

himself into the fight for change. His radicalism made him one of Brighton's strongest proponents for reform and he often stood far to the left of his fellow liberals. For example, the act of reform was accompanied and fuelled by an increasing awareness of Britain's high unemployment and poor population. The country was swept by arson attacks, usually aimed at the landed classes - barns and rural buildings were favourite targets. Eighteen of the leading citizens of Hove met at the Keriston Arms in Waterloo Street near the end of November 1830 to discuss how best to protect their area and its farming properties from incendiaries. A resolution was drawn up and published in the local newspapers condemning the violence and pledging the organisation of a special patrol to apprehend offenders. Everyone at the meeting voted in favour of the move. There was only one dissenting vote - from Busby.(101)

With the political debate reaching a feverish pitch, a larger meeting of Brighton's citizens was held at the Old Ship Tavern on 18 February 1831. The townsmen passed many resolutions that night, including one to petition both Houses of Parliament for reform. Their demands were strong: reduction in taxes; the abolition of a number of offensive political offices; a decrease in the army; the procurement of certain church property by the nation; and the right of every householder to be given a balloted vote. Busby was one of the seven-member committee charged with gathering signatures.(102) Within the month, 6700 names accompanied Brighton's petition to Westminster.(103)

Busby's prominent involvement in local

72
Lansdowne Square, Hove. A secluded little square dominated by a large town house façade.

activities during the reform period, his service as a Commissioner on the Brunswick Estate, and his election as a vestryman for Hove, enhanced his political image considerably.(104) The time had finally arrived when to be an outspoken radical was not only accepted, but praised. In recognition of his services, Busby's fellow citizens bestowed upon him the honorary position of High Commissioner of Hove.(105)

After a bitter struggle, the great Reform Act was passed in June 1832. The register for Brighton and Hove could now boast about 250 men eligible to vote in the reforming election(106) - still an insignificant number considering that the population was estimated at nearly 38,000.(107) But as a property owner, Charles Augustin Busby was amongst the few. Like his 15 fellow voters in Hove he was, of course, to vote Independent.(108)

Six months after moving to Brunswick Town, Busby made one final attempt at redeveloping the seafront property to the west of Brunswick Town. The land had now passed into the hands of the financier Issac Lyon Goldsmid. Repeating his idea of the three consecutive squares on the Wick Road, Busby suggested widening and increasing the depth of each square.(109) (Fig.71) In fact, they less resembled squares than 75 foot wide cul-de-sacs similar to Cavendish Place.

Goldsmid chose another architect, Decimus Burton, who in the same year, 1830, designed Queen Adelaide's Crescent.(110) Construc-

73
Nos. 13 & 15 Lansdowne Place, Hove. The fine sets of semi-detached villas on Lansdowne Place were Busby's last buildings.

tion began on the south-east houses of the Crescent, opposite the end of Brunswick Terrace, in late 1831.(111) But after the completion of only ten houses, the whole scheme was suspended for 15 to 20 years, and then completed in a slightly modified form.(112)

Busby did, however, manage to design one of his three projected squares on the Wick Road, Lansdowne Square, and the houses opposite his own residence. The small square has a fine façade as its focal point, a miniature Portland House. (Fig.72) Also on Lansdowne Place, Busby introduced semi-detached villas, (Fig.73) a change from the long lines of terrace housing in Brunswick Town. He probably also designed the three houses at Nos.25-29 Lansdowne Place.

In 1825 Busby had given a lecture on mechanics at the newly founded Brighton Mechanics' Institution at 31 West Street.(113) But over the years the Institution had flagged for lack of funds, and the premises had been sold and converted into a grocer's shop.(114) But by the end of the decade, with the principal part of his work on Brunswick Town completed, Busby found the time to turn a greater part of his attention to scientific study and experiment. He followed with interest the fate of a local inventor, John Vallance junior, who unsuccessfully attempted to build a pneumatic railway between Brighton and its harbour five miles away at Shoreham.(115)

And he returned to his New York experiments in steam-powered navigation. His

74
Design for a steamboat propellant mechanism, *c*1832. Being near the sea made it easier for Busby to continue his experiments begun in America in steam-powered navigation.

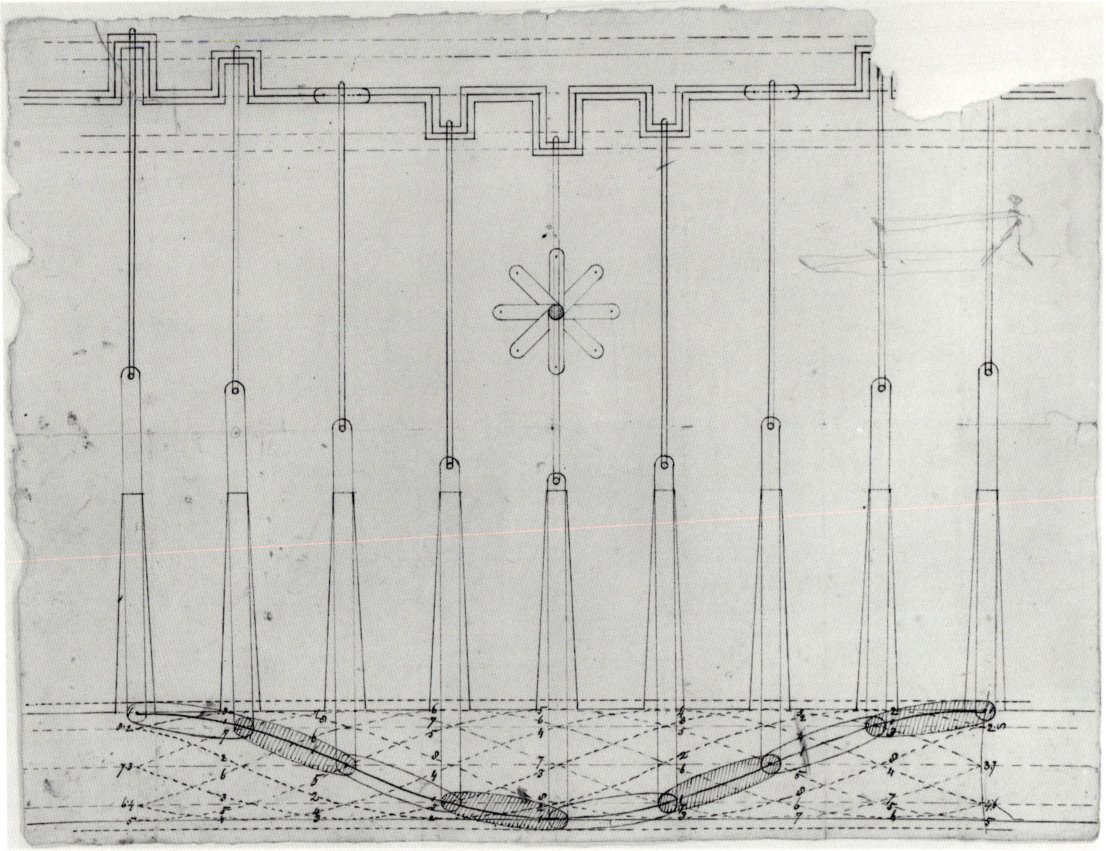

American waterwheel having proved ineffective, he set about devising an alternative method of propulsion. He invented a system whereby a boat might be propelled by piston rods activating a linked series of underwater paddles in a rotational motion.(116) (Fig.74) And in May 1832, he and a group of his friends successfully navigated a small boat, five feet wide by twenty feet long, along the coast from Brunswick Terrace to beyond Kemp Town, manoeuvring around several sailboats and shooting past all the other vessels. The waterwheels were said to be fixed to the boat "in a novel and peculiar manner," and so constructed as not to drag in the water if the sails were used.(117)

Out of Busby's steamboat activities emerged his most far-fetched but ingenious scheme. In May 1829 he made a plan for converting the moat, by then a dry ditch, around the Tower of London "into a capacious steam boat dock".(118) (Fig.75) Busby proposed widening and deepening the moat to allow room for 15 steamboats to berth. The

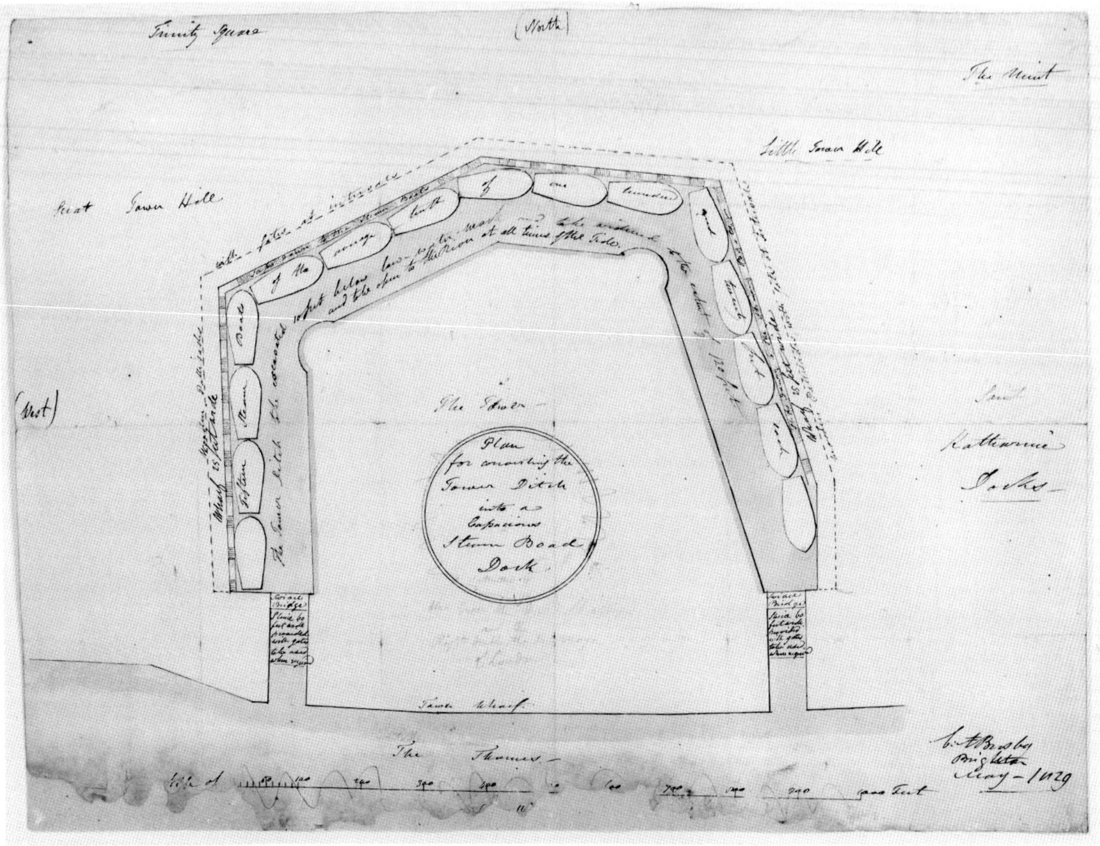

75
Unexecuted plan for a steamboat dock surrounding the Tower of London, 1829. Busby proposed converting the dry moat into a berth for steamboats.

inner dock was to have been open to the river when the tide was high, and controlled by sluices at other times. Excited by the scheme's chances of success, Busby submitted his plan to the Prime Minister - the Duke of Wellington - and to the Lord Mayor of London. The idea was not pursued.

When in 1824 the plans for building Brunswick Town were first released to the public, it was stated that all of the houses on the estate were to have hot and cold running water.(119) It proved an unfulfilled promise. But Busby was actively seeking a method of circulating heated water, and in 1832 he took out a patent for an improved means of central heating.(120) At the centre of his system was a steam engine, which Busby christened the "Volcanic", that by means of the smoke from the fire heating the water turned a circulating mechanism to send the hot water *below* the furnace.(121) Busby made a tin model of the Volcanic and set it up in the Holborn premises of an ironmonger named Eckstein. It attracted approval from such famous scientists as Michael Faraday and Dionysius Lardner.(122) J.C. Loudon also studied Busby's system to see how it might effectively be used in heating conservatories. Busby's invention was so well received that when in 1832 the central police station in Bow Street was built, 12 cells were heated by his method using the waiting room fire which stood 120 feet away and 12 feet below the cells.(123)

Busby's reputation as an hydraulic engineer grew. For several weeks he wrote a series of highly detailed reports about Ericsson's steam engine in the pages of the *Mechanics' Magazine*.(124) And it was no doubt Busby who encouraged Walter Hancock to travel down to Brighton in his steam-carriage, the "Infant". Busby met Hancock on his thundering coke-fed contraption eight miles outside of town on the London Road, on top of Pyecombe Hill, from where they descended at a heady speed of 13 mph, entering Brighton at 10 mph. A large crowd turned out and gave them three hearty cheers. "The experiment," wrote Busby, "is considered here as a very satisfactory proof of the practicability of travelling by steam on *common* roads."(125)

Sadly, a few months later, Busby's world came crashing down around him. On 4 February 1833, he had to play-act a humiliating scene. Leaving his house he was met by a friend, the builder John Manley. "How do you do Manley," Busby greeted him, "I am rather in a hurry. I am going to take the coach to avoid being arrested by Mr Bennett."(126) It was a charade that, by law, had to be enacted: Busby had to be seen avoiding his creditors so that they could instigate bankruptcy proceedings against him.

Busby's property speculations had failed miserably. He held 85 debts and owed more than £12,600, most of it to his backers on the final wing of Brunswick Terrace. But his smaller investments had also helped bring him down. There was the mortgage on his house, two house carcasses in Waterloo Street, seven houses in the Western Buildings on Sillwood Road, leasehold of ground in Montpelier Road from Kemp, and three freehold plots of ground in Park Crescent in Worthing upon which A.H. Wilds was in the process of building. And then there were the sad personal debts: £50 to his brother Julian Busby; the £320 premium and stamp duty paid for articling his son to Jacob Boys; the wages due to his servants Elizabeth Roberts and Ann Ingram; and even the unpaid bill to his cheesemonger Joseph Jenkinson of North Street, purveyor of reindeer tongues.

His creditors and friends rallied round and took it upon themselves to sort out his affairs. In the end, after all his assets were realised, the books balanced. But Busby and his family were left penniless. As freeholder on their house, the Reverend Scutt generously allowed them to remain in Stanhope Place.

Despite this setback, Busby lost none of his enthusiasm for undertaking new schemes and research. When on 30 August 1833, the large domed conservatory near Brunswick Town called the Anthaeum collapsed, Busby volunteered to supervise its re-erection.(127) And later that year, he filed a long report attributing the extensive storm damage wreaked upon the Chain Pier not to the action of the wind as commonly believed, but to lightning.(128)

He kept up a lively correspondence in the *Mechanics' Magazine*, describing in one issue the unusual sighting of a bright light in the heavens one September evening as he looked out his window in Stanhope Place,(129) and in another, his theory on the magnetism of the planet's rotation.(130)

In January 1834, Busby delivered a series of lectures on astronomy in the Brighton Town Hall, illustrating his talk with a demonstration of his hydraulic orrery. The audience was enthralled by its beauty.(131)

During his astronomy lectures Busby spoke quietly and sometimes inaudibly, perhaps a sign of ill health. He died on 18 September 1834, at his Stanhope Place residence.(132) The funeral took place a week later, on 25 September, at the old parish church of St Andrew, Hove.(133) Busby was buried in the graveyard. He left an estate of less than £200.(134)

After Busby's death, Brunswick Town was not completed for several decades. Imitations of his bow fronted terrace houses were continued up Lansdowne Place, across Western Road and into Upper Brunswick Place. Streets of similar terraces were extended both east and west. Loosely speaking, this whole area of cream-stuccoed terraces is now known as Brunswick Town, extending over its formal boundaries. So strong had been Busby's original concept that his style of Regency architecture continued to be built for many decades after his death, far into the reign of Queen Victoria.

NOTES

ABBREVIATIONS

Btn Gaz	*Brighton Gazette*
Btn Hld	*Brighton Herald*
Cowdry	Mary Bartlett Cowdry, *American Academy of Fine Arts and American Art-Union*, XIX (New York, 1953)
Dale	Antony Dale, *Fashionable Brighton* (1947, 2nd edition 1967)
ESCRO	East Sussex Country Record Office, Lewes
Graves	Algernon Graves, *The Royal Academy of Arts: A Complete Dictionary of Contributors and their Work from its Foundation in 1769 to 1904* (1905), 8 vols
N-YHS	New-York Historical Society, New York
RA	Royal Academy of Arts, London
RIBA DC	Royal Institute of British Architects, Drawings Collection, London
Soane	Sir John Soane's Museum, London
V&A	Victoria and Albert Museum, London

Unless otherwise noted, the place of publication is London.

CHAPTER 1
EARLY LIFE AND CAREER 1786-1817

1 V&A: Registered Papers for Mrs K.E. Barnes, 1936-38.
2 A complete list of Thomas Busby's compositions appears in his entry in *The New Grove Dictionary of Music*, III (1980), p.497.
3 [T. Busby], "Dr. Busby" in *Public Characters of 1802-03* (1803), p.382; K.G.F. Spence in his article "The Learned Dr Busby" in *Music and Letters*, XXXVII, April 1956, pp.141-43 draws almost wholly from *Public Characters.*
4 *Public Characters*, p.378.
5 *Survey of London*, XXXI (1963), p.245.
6 As noted in the preface to Thomas Busby's translation of *The Nature of Things by Lucretius* (1813).
7 *The Dictionary of Architecture*, Wyatt Papworth, ed., I (1877 edition), p.38.
8 Robert Thorne, "Rebirth of a Rogue: Origins of the Skin Floor" in *Architects' Journal*, CLXXXVIII, 23 July 1986, pp.29-38.
9 George H. Chettle, *The Queen's House, Greenwich*, 14th monograph of the London Survey Committee (n.d.).
10 RA: Registrar of Probationers.
11 RIBA DC: N25/2.
12 Graves, I, pp.360-61.
13 RIBA DC: N25/1.
14 RIBA DC: N25/7 (1-2).
15 RIBA DC: N25/3 (1-11).
16 East Croydon Public Library, Reference Section: Abstract of the Minutes of the Corporation for the Management of Waste Lands in the Parish of Croydon, Dec 1807. The architect Samual Pepys Cockerell (1753-1827) received the commission, but the scheme was not built as it was deemed too expensive.
17 V&A: P42-1936.
18 RA: Minutes of the General Assembly of Royal Academicians, II. Meeting of 10 Dec 1807.
19 *The Diary of Joseph Farington*, Kathryn Cave, ed., VIII, July 1806 - Dec 1807, (1982), pp.3159-62.
20 RA: Royal Academy Schools Chronological Record.
21 Busby's fellow members from Alexander's office were William Hurst Ashipital (1776-1852), George Smith (1783-1869), and John Wallen (1785-1865); and at the Royal Academy Schools, Edmund Aikin (1780-1820), Charles S. Smith (c1790- ?), and James George Bubb (1782-1853).
22 *Essays of the London Architectural Society*, 2 vols. (1808 & 1810), p.iv.
23 C.A. Busby, *A Series of Designs, etc.* (1808), p.13.
24 RIBA DC: N25/14; N25/15.
25 *A Series of Designs, etc.*, p.18.
26 Graves, I, p.360; RIBA DC: N25/11 (1-3).
27 Graves, I, p.360.
28 *Bristol Journal* 16 Dec 1809.
29 John Latimer, *The Annuals of Bristol* (Bristol, 1887), p.32.
30 Soane: Letter Book, 17 Feb 1802 - Nov 1815. Letter from Soane to

Busby (copy), 28 Oct 1809.
31 Soane: Private Correspondence, I.B.23.2. Letter from Busby to Soane, 31 Oct 1809.
32 Bristol Public Library: B3961, newspaper clipping.
33 Bristol Record Office: Commercial Coffee Room Committee Record Book 1808-18.
34 Bryan Little, "Restoring a Grecian Masterpiece: The Commercial Rooms, Bristol" in *Country Life*, CLX, 23 Sept 1976, pp.831-32.
35 Bristol Record Office: Commercial Coffee Room, Proceedings of General Meetings, 1808-1945.
36 Thomas Busby, *Concert Room etc.*, I, pp.3-4.
37 RIBA DC: N25/42 (2-4).
38 Graves, I, p.361; RIBA DC: N25/20.
39 *Victoria History of the Counties of England: Berkshire*, IV (1924), p.59. Wasey was a bachelor who was later to gain a spot of notoriety for attempting to create as his heirs two boys he had discovered making sand castles on the beach at Southsea who were coincidentally also named Wasey.
40 RIBA DC: N25/19.
41 *Warwick Advertiser*, 9 Feb 1811.
42 RIBA DC: N25/6 (1-3).
43 *The Gentleman's Magazine*, LXXXII (part 2), July 1812, p.80.
44 Robin Evans, *The Fabrication of Virtue: English Prison Architecture 1750-1840* (Cambridge, 1982), pp.244-45.
45 Jeremy Bentham, *Panopticon or the Inspection House* (1791); also see Thomas A. Markus, "Pattern of the Law" in *Architectural Review*, CXVI, Oct 1954, pp.251-56.
46 George Holford, *An Account of the General Penitentiary at Millbank* (1828).
47 RIBA DC: N25/25.
48 See M.H. Tomlinson, *Victorian Prisons: Administration and Architecture 1835-1877*, Ph.D. thesis, University of London, 1975.
49 Bristol Record Office: Plan Book E, p.91.
50 Bristol Record Office: Plan Book E, p.90.
51 George Gilbert Scott, *Personal and Professional Recollections* (1879), pp.63-64.
52 Bethnal Green Museum (V&A): E4910-1923.
53 Graves, V, p.169.
54 PRO: RAIL 860/5. Letter from Busby to the Committee of the Regents Canal Company, 2 Nov 1812. (I would like to thank Dennis Smith for bringing this source to my attention.)
55 As above.
56 C.A. Busby, "A Statement of the Proceedings before His Majesty's Commissioners for Building Additional Churches, and other Persons, in Relation to the Intended Churches at Leeds, and Oldham, 1821, 1822" (1822). Copies of this broadsheet are in the Soane: Private Correspondence, I.B.23.11; and the National Art Library, V&A, in Box I.35.J.
57 Patent No.3683; RIBA DC: N25/102 (4).
58 Christopher Hussey, "Somerley, Hampshire: The Seat of the Earl of Normanton" in *Country Life*, CXXIII, 16, 23 & 30 Jan 1958, pp.108-11, 156-59, 202-05.
59 For similar schemes, see G. Carter, P. Goode and K. Laurie, *Humphrey Repton, Landscape Gardener, 1752-1818* (Sainsbury Centre for Visual Arts, 1982).
60 There are four drawings for the Somerley garden building in the possession of the Earl of Normanton: (1) Site plan, dated Sept 1814 (2) Ground plan of pheasantry, dated March 1815 (3) Perspective of pheasantry, dated March 1815 (Fig.20) (4) Working detail of iron arches.
61 Edward Hubbard, *The Buildings of Wales: Clwyd* (Harmondsworth, Middlesex, 1986), pp.175-76.
62 National Library of Wales: Department of Prints and Maps, Box 1037.
63 As above.
64 As above.
65 As above.
66 RIBA DC: N25/27 (1-3).
67 RIBA DC: N25/28 (1-3).
68 Edmund Buthcher, *The Sidmouth Guide* (1818), p.30.
69 Sidmouth Museum: 2 prints by John Wallis of Powys Cottage, one dated 1 Jan 1819 & the other 4 April 1826.
70 Soane: Private Correspondence, I.B.23.12.
71 Church Building Commission: Minute Book 6. Francis Goodwin to Church Building Commissioners, 4 Feb 1822.
72 R.J.M. Sutherland, F Eng.BA.FICE.FI Struct E., "Assessment of the structural adequacy of the early 19th century roof truss designed by C. Busby etc", Report dated 23 July 1989.
73 *The Gentleman's Magazine*, LXXI (part 2), p.84.
74 Greater London Record Office: P89/MRY 1.
75 As above.

CHAPTER 2
IN AMERICA 1817-1819

1 C.A. Busby, *An Essay on the Propulsion of Navigable Bodies* (June 1818), p.1.
2 Cowdry, p.52.
3 R.W.G. Vail, *Knickerbocker Birthday: A Sesqui-Centennial History of the New-York Historical Society, 1804-1954* (New York, 1954), pp.48-49.
4 N-YHS: Minute Book of the Historical Society, New-York Institution, p.89.
5 N-YHS: Minute Book of the American Academy of Fine Arts, III, p.18.

6 N-YHS: Minute Book of the Literary and Philosophical Society of New-York, p.93.
7 Archives of American Art, Smithsonian Institution, Washington: D23, 341-342, Robert Graham Collection. Letter dated 28 Feb 1817.
8 See Irma B. Jaffe, *John Trumbull: Patriot-Artist of the American Revolution* (New York, 1975).
9 Cowdry, p.52.
10 N-YHS: Minute Book of the Historical Society, New-York Institution, p.101.
11 N-YHS: Department of Prints and Drawings.
12 Robert C. Alberts, *Benjamin West, A Biography* (Boston, 1978), pp.348-55, 378.
13 Pennsylvania Hospital, Philadelphia: Letter from West to Coates, 2 March 1817.
14 Historical Society of Pennsylvania, Philadelphia: Bb615/P384.
15 This drawing was sold at Sotheby's New York, 30 June 1984 to the Hirschl & Adler Gallery of New York, who subsequently sold it on to an unknown source.
16 Pennsylvania Hospital, Philadelphia: Report on the Committee on the Building for Wests' Picture etc. 1 Jan 1818.
17 RIBA DC: N25/31 (1-7).
18 James G. Scott and Edward A. Wyatt, *Petersburg's Story: A History* (Petersburg, Virginia, 1960), p.149. The theatre survived until the early part of this century, having been rebuilt after a fire in 1850.
19 Busby, *Navigable Bodies*, pp.1-2.
20 N-YHS: Minute Book of the Literary and Philosophical Society of New-York, p.98.
21 Busby, *Navigable Bodies*, p.14.
22 *London Journal of Arts and Sciences*, I (1820), pp.341-44, & plate XIV. Patent to Samuel Lambert, of Princes's Street, Leicester Square, for an invention of an improved waterwheel, applicable to Mills and Navigable Bodies.
23 N-YHS: Minutes of the Literary and Philosophical Society of New-York, p.93.
24 RIBA DC: N25/34.
25 RIBA DC: N25/32.
26 RIBA DC: N25/33.
27 RIBA DC: N25/29.
28 See Robert L. Alexander, "The Young Professional in Philadelphia and Baltimore, 1808-20" in *Robert Mills, Architect*, John M. Bryan, ed. (Washington, 1989), pp.60-62.
29 C.A. Busby, "A Statement...Leeds, and Oldham".
30 RIBA DC: N25/30.
31 Matthew Roth, *Connecticut: An Inventory of Historic Engineering and Industrial Sites* (Washington, 1981), p.36.
32 Busby's engravings are discussed and illustrated in Glenn Brown, *History of the United States Capitol* (Washington, 1900), I, p.56, & plates 71 & 72.
33 Soane: Private Correspondence, I.B.23.9 & .10. Two explanatory sheets from Busby, May 1821.
34 N-YHS: Minutes of the American Academy of Fine Arts, p.67.
35 N-YHS: Minutes of the Literary and Philosophical Society of New-York, p.97.
36 Massachusetts Historical Society, Boston: Print Department.
37 Historical Society of Pennsylvania, Philadelphia: Simon Gratz Autograph Collection. Receipts dated 20 June 1818 and 6 September 1822.
38 Cowdrey, p.52.
39 N-YHS: American Academy of Fine Arts, I, document 45.
40 Cowdrey, p.52.

CHAPTER 3
RETURN TO ENGLAND 1820-1823

1 All references to Busby and the Church Commissioners, unless otherwise noted, are derived from the Church Commissioners: His Majesty's Commissioners of Building New Churches, Minute Books Nos. 5 & 6; A full and detailed account of the conflict between Busby and Goodwin is given by Michael Port, "Francis Goodwin (1784-1835): An Architect of the 1820s: A Study of his Relationship with the Church Building Commissioners and his Quarrel with C.A. Busby" in *Architectural History*, I (1958), pp.60-72.
2 C.A. Busby, "A Statement...Leeds and Oldham.
3 Soane: Private Correspondence, I.B.23.6. Letter from Busby to Soane, 1 Jan 1822.
4 C.A. Busby, "A Statement...Leeds, and Oldham".
5 RIBA DC: N25/36 (1-9).
6 John Dearing, *Saint Mary's: The Borough Church of Maidenhead* (Maidenhead, 1981).
7 London (City). Court of Common Council. Committee for Rebuilding London Bridge, 1823.
8 The Rittenhouse Orrery is still on display in the Library of the University of Pennsylvania, Philadelphia.
9 *Transactions of the Society of Arts*, XL, 1823, pp.98-104.
10 *Mechanics' Magazine*, XIV, 4 Dec 1830, pp.241-42; XV, 26 March 1831, pp.57-58; Busby's hydraulic orrery is discussed and illustrated in Henry C. King, *Geared to the Stars: The Evolution of Planetariums, Orreries, and Astronomical Clocks* (Bristol, 1978), pp.339-40.
11 The orrery was probably disposed of sometime in the last century.

CHAPTER 4
BRIGHTON & HOVE 1823-1834

1 See F.H. Kemp, *A General History of the Kemp and Kemp Families of Great Britain and Her Colonies* (1902): also Clifford Musgrave, *Life in Brighton* (revised edition 1981).
2 *Btn Gaz*, 5 April 1827.
3 All but two of the houses in Waterloo Place, including Busby's residence, were destroyed in 1968-70.
4 See Hermoine Hobhouse, *Thomas Cubitt: Master Builder* (1971), pp.361-72; There is a design for a "Cornice, Kemp Town, 1832" by J.G. Crace in the RIBA DC: John Gregory Crace Album, folio 18.
5 5 Geo. IV, c.11. 3 June 1824.
6 PRO: CO323/144, record drawing of St George's Chapel, made by Busby and sent to Lord Charles Somerset, Governor of Cape Colony, Sept 1826.
7 *Btn Gaz*, 10 April 1828.
8 RIBA DC: N25/63.
9 *Btn Gaz*, 25 March 1824; see also Michael Gray, *A Study of the Work of Amon Wilds and Charles Augustus Busby, in Brunswick Town, Hove. 1823-1834*, Architecture thesis, Brighton Polytechnic, 1989 for excellent descriptions and measured drawings of buildings in Brunswick Town; also John Pareas, *Busby: The Neglected One*, Architecture thesis, Brighton Polytechnic, 1973.
10 *Btn Gaz*, 14 Sept 1826.
11 *Btn Gaz*, 23 Oct 1828.
12 RIBA DC: N25/60.
13 *Btn Gaz*, 15 Sept 1825.
14 *Btn Gaz*, 23 Oct 1828; Portland House survives today as Pearson House, stripped of its portico and heavily rebuilt.
15 ESCRO: Brighton Commissioners Minute Book, 1827-29. At a meeting of 11 June 1828, Major Russell requested the installation of gas lighting for Portland Place.
16 Graves, I, p.361.
17 *Btn Gaz*, 11 June 1825.
18 In the collection of the Royal Pavilion, Art Gallery and Museum, Brighton.
19 *Btn Gaz*, 3 March 1825; RIBA DC: N25/113 (1-2).
20 Auction particulars, with the auctioneer's handwritten notes, are held in a private collection.
21 RIBA DC: N25/38 (1-5).
22 ESCRO: HOW 37/1-3. Correspondence relating to the building of St Peter's Church, Brighton.
23 *Btn Gaz*, 21 Aug 1823.
24 *Btn Gaz*, 10 March 1825.
25 *Btn Hld*, 2 April 1825.
26 *Btn Gaz*, 19 April 1827.
27 *Btn Gaz*, 10 July 1828.
28 *Btn Gaz*, 30 Dec 1824.
29 *Btn Gaz*, 3 June 1824.
30 *Btn Gaz*, 6 & 20 May 1824.
31 *Btn Gaz*, 20 May 1824; *Btn Gaz*, 11 Nov 1830 & 10 Feb 1831. A.H. Wilds introduced additional interior columns in 1830-31, to "give an appearance of strength and solidity to the buiding."
32 In the collection of the Royal Pavilion, Art Gallery and Museum, Brighton. The maker's mark, "WC" in an oblong band, probably refers to the London silversmith William Chawner II (died 1834); *Btn Gaz*, 20 Jan 1825; *Btn Hld*, 15 Jan 1825.
33 RIBA DC: N25/37; *The Clerical Guide* (1822).
34 *Btn Gaz*, 17 March 1825.
35 *Btn Gaz*, 21 April 1825.
36 *Btn Gaz*, 4 Aug 1825; Engraved by W. Alexander with the inscription "H. Wilds, Architect, Brighton".
37 *Btn Gaz*, 7 April 1825.
38 Dale, pp.30-31, undertakes an attribution of undocumented Wilds and Busby buildings in Brighton. Dale's list is unimpeachable.
39 *Btn Gaz*, 29 July 1824.
40 Graves, VIII, p.266.
41 Graves, I, p.361. This is the only instance in which Busby's name preceeded that of Wilds.
42 *London Gazette*, 9 Aug 1825, p.1398.
43 *Btn Gaz*, 5 April 1827.
44 RIBA DC: N25/55 (1-6).
45 *Btn Gaz*, 16 April 1829.
46 *Btn Gaz*, 11 Aug 1825; Grenville Place was demolished to make for Churchill Square, *c*1966.
47 RIBA DC: S10/56 (1-2), SOS/A/3 (1-2).
48 RIBA DC: N25/74 (1).
49 RIBA DC: N25/94 (left side); Collection of James Griffiths (right side).
50 RIBA DC: N25/93.
51 RIBA DC: N25/66.
52 RIBA DC: N25/61 (1).
53 RIBA DC: N25/72 (3), N25/73, N25/87 (5), N25/90 (1).
54 ESCRO: Brighton Commissioners Minute Book 1827-29. Letter dated 5 March 1828.
55 RIBA DC: N25/85 (1-4).
56 RIBA DC: N25/68.
57 See ESCRO: HIL6/56. An indentured contract selling 8 Brunswick Place on 10 Oct 1829, releasing the previous indenture of 7 July 1826.
58 ESCRO: LT Hove. Land tax books, 1780-1831.
59 *Btn Hld*, 4 June 1825.
60 RIBA DC: N25/75 (1-2).
61 Dale, p.119.
62 Then No.35. All houses in Brunswick Square were renumbered in Dec 1834. ("The houses in Brunswick Square being irregularly numbered in consequence of two additional houses having been erected since the original plan of the Square was prepared." from Hove Borough Council: Minute Book of the Commissioners for the Brunswick Estate, p.201).
63 RIBA DC: John Gregory Crace Album, folio 10. The accompanying designs for three dados and a ceiling rose may also have been for Heaviside.

64 *Btn Gaz*, 6 Aug 1829.
65 *Btn Hld*, 4 June 1825.
66 RIBA DC: N25/61 (2).
67 RIBA DC: N25/76.
68 RIBA DC: N25/95.
69 RIBA DC: N25/79-81.
70 RIBA DC: N25/82.
71 *Btn Gaz*, 14 Sept 1826.
72 RIBA DC: N25/78 (1-4).
73 *Btn Gaz*, 23 March & 27 April 1826.
74 *Btn Hld*, 3 March 1827.
75 *Btn Gaz*, 21 Aug 1828.
76 *Btn Gaz*, 18 Oct, 27 Nov & 4 Dec 1828.
77 *Btn Gaz*, 31 May 1827.
78 *Btn Gaz*, 15 Feb 1827.
79 *Btn Gaz*, 5 April 1827.
80 *Btn Gaz*, 18 Aug 1827.
81 *Btn Hld*, 9 June 1827. The esplanade was designed by A.H. Wilds.
82 PRO: Bankruptcy Records, B3/738.
83 *Btn Gaz*, 18 Oct 1827.
84 *Btn Hld*, 15 Sept 1827.
85 RIBA DC: N25/92 (1-2).
86 RIBA DC: N25/70 (1-9).
87 A hotel was built on the garden in the Victorian period.
88 RIBA DC: N25/90 (5).
89 ESCRO: Brighton Commissioners Book 1827-29. Meeting of 23 July 1828; PRO: B3/738; RIBA DC: N25/ 90 (4).
90 ESCRO: HOW 27/23. Rent Account Book of T.R. Kemp, 1826-31.
91 RIBA DC: N25/71 (1).
92 Historical Society of Pennsylvania, Philadelphia: Simon Gratz Autograph Collection.
93 *Btn Gaz*, 31 Dec 1829.
94 11 Geo. IV, c.16. 8 April 1830.
95 Busby was elected a Commissioner on 27 July 1830. See Hove Borough Council: Minute Book of the Commissioners for the Brunswick Estate, p.26.
96 RIBA DC: N25/106.
97 *Btn Gaz*, 5 April 1827.
98 Hove Borough Council: Minute Book of the Commissioners for the Brunswick Estate, p.143.
99 *London Gazette*, 11 July 1834, p.1321; 17 Oct 1834, p.1860; 2 Dec 1834, p.2223; I would like to thank Derek Oakensen and Michael Ray for bringing Clisby's bankruptcy to my attention.
100 See Antony Dale, *Brighton Town and Brighton People* (1976), pp.69-81.
101 *Btn Gaz*, 25 Nov 1830.
102 *Btn Gaz*, 24 Feb 1831. Thomas Cooper, architect of Brighton Town Hall, was also on the signature committee.
103 *Btn Gaz*, 24 March 1831.
104 ESCRO: PAR 387/12/1. Hove Vestry Minute Book.
105 *Btn Hld*, 24 Aug 1831. As High Commissioner, Busby had to deal with a cholera scare in Nov 1831. See *Btn Hld*, 26 Nov 1831.
106 *Btn Gaz*, 6 Sept 1832.
107 *Btn Gaz*, 3 June 1831. The figure was taken from the 1831 Census.
108 ESCRO: East Sussex Poll, 1832, p.42.
109 RIBA DC: N25/74 (2).
110 RIBA DC: XOS/A/1.
111 *Btn Gaz*, 30 Nov 1831.
112 See Dale, pp.149-53.
113 *Btn Hld*, 19 Nov & 10 Dec 1825.
114 *Btn Hld*, 19 Nov 1825.
115 *Btn Gaz*, 7 June 1827.
116 RIBA DC: N25/99.
117 *Btn Gaz*, 30 May 1832; RIBA DC: N25/100.
118 RIBA DC: N25/98.
119 *Btn Gaz*, 25 March 1824.
120 Patent 6268, 6 July 1832.
121 *Mechanics' Magazine*, XVI, 4 Feb 1832, pp.329-30.
122 Lardner and Busby probably knew one another as their scientific interests were similar, especially in the field of hydraulics and the motion of the planets. Moreover, Lardner was carrying on an affair with Mrs Heaviside of 15 Brunswick Square, who he was to elope with in 1840. Captain Heaviside's revenge made the affair a public scandal.
123 *Btn Gaz*, 16 Aug 1832.
124 *Mechanics' Magazine*, XVIII, 6, 13 & 20 Oct, 3 Nov 1832, pp.5, 20-22, 39, 72.
125 *Mechanics' Magazine*, XVIII, 10 Nov 1832, pp.84-85.
126 PRO: B3/738; *London Gazette*, 9 April 1833, pp.693-94.
127 Dale, pp.154-55.
128 John Bruce, *The History of Brighton with the Latest Improvements, to 1836* (Brighton, 1836), pp.99-101.
129 *Mechanics' Magazine*, XX, 12 Oct 1833, p.25.
130 *Mechanics' Magazine*, XXI, 17 May 1834, pp.104-05.
131 *Btn Gaz*, 16 & 23 Jan 1834.
132 *Gentleman's Magazine*, CIV (part 2), Oct 1834, p.446.
133 ESCRO: Register of Burials in the Parish of Hove. Busby's middle name was incorrectly recorded as "Augustus", an error which was perpetuated by later historians.
134 ESCRO: B22/199.

INDEX

Numbers in italics refer to illustration page numbers. Roman numerals refer to colour plates.

Printed by Expression Printers Ltd, London N7